YOU WHO?

WHY YOU MATTER AND HOW TO DEAL WITH IT

Rachel Jankovic

canonpress
Moscow, Idaho

Published by Canon Press
P.O. Box 8729, Moscow, Idaho 83843
800.488.2034 | www.canonpress.com

Cover design by James Engerbretson
Interior design by Valerie Anne Bost

Printed in the United States of America.

Library of Congress Cataloging-in-Publication Data:
Names: Jankovic, Rachel, author.
Title: You Who? Why You Matter and How to Deal with It / by Rachel Jankovic.
Description: Moscow, Idaho : Canon Press, [2018]
Identifiers: LCCN 2018024679 | ISBN 9781947644885 (pbk.)
Subjects: LCSH: Identity (Psychology)--Religious aspects--Christianity.
Classification: LCC BV4509.5 .J36 2018 | DDC 233--dc23
LC record available at https://lccn.loc.gov/2018024679

18 19 20 21 22 23 24   9 8 7 6 5 4 3 2 1

From the end of the earth I will cry to You,
When my heart is overwhelmed;
Lead me to the rock that is higher than I.
-Psalm 61:2

To Morgan,
a faithful lighthouse on that higher rock.

CONTENTS

1

TROUBLE, TRUTH, AND GLORY

PERHAPS I SHOULD OPEN THIS BOOK with a warning. If you are looking for a book that will gently pet your bangs and soothe your worried brow, telling you how beautiful you are, this is not it. I will not stick only to the feel-good themes and ways to boost your confidence, telling you that you (no matter what you are doing at the moment) are *enough*. I will not give you a big pep talk about how to fight for *you*, and there is no chapter on morning affirmations.

This book is not here to help you in your quest for self-love. I want something much, much better for you, because I want something *true* for you.

purpose of book

The goal of this book is to encourage and equip believing women to see their identity in Christ as the most essential part of them, and to see all the ways that will work its way out in their lives, manifesting itself as strength, dignity, and clarity of purpose.

My goal here is not mere hard words for the sake of hard words, but rather hard words so we can embrace the glorious Good News. We cannot have the one without the other. There is no need for good news if we will not see the problem of sin. When we want to celebrate what God has done for us, we need to look honestly at why we needed it in the first place and what we are without it. If you won't face the fact that we have sin, there will be no joy in looking to a Savior.

My grandpa has always said that soft teaching makes hard hearts and hard teaching makes soft hearts. When we encourage each other with platitudes about our self-worth and our beauty, we are simply lying for the sake of *feelings*. When we accustom ourselves to soft lies so we won't feel affronted, we become a hard-hearted people.

Ironically, the harder we try to make ourselves feel better, the further we remove ourselves from the one true comfort in this life. Our pain will only grow. We need comfort more and more, but we are taking away all hope of comfort by looking to ourselves for salvation. We are turning ourselves into a bunch of brittle, crackling liars who do nothing but affirm each other. There is no actual joy or peace here—just an endless quest to feel better, and maybe some throw pillows telling us we are beautiful.

On the other hand, when we are willing to face the hard truths about who we are and what our purpose is, we will not become a bunch of hard-hearted robots without feelings. Rather, our hearts will be soft, and our feelings will be rightly ordered, not defending us from God but making us run to Him. We will become much more real, much more tender Christian women. We can encourage each other without lying. We can receive encouragement that is true and actually life giving. Without our self-protecting goggles on, we are free to rightly see our Savior, the source of all true encouragement.

When we love the Good News, we will willingly endure the hard words. When we discard the hard words to protect our feelings, we will find that we have also discarded the Good News.

Parts of this book will be all about trouble. The trouble with us. The trouble with what we have been taught. The trouble with how we try to find out who we are and what we are for. The trouble with what our unbelieving culture has made normal. The trouble with our philosophical heritage (mostly those existentialists). The trouble with sin. The trouble with our broken relationship with God. The trouble with our attempts to self-flatter our way out of it. The trouble with self-worship and the trouble with soft words. Truth-telling doesn't always go down easy, but when it finally does, the dying patient gets better.

But in every case where we look honestly at the trouble, we will be equipped to see the truth and the glory that the trouble has kept us from. It is not enough to simply reject falsehoods; we must grab onto truth in their place. We don't want to simply get the rank stench of unbelief out—we want to bring the sweet aroma of truth in.

As a young child I could not decide whether to be a missionary or a cheerleader when I grew up. I remember the hilarity that broke out when I earnestly placed this struggle before my family, looking for feedback. Strangely, much of my life (and this book!) represents a little bit of both. I love the Gospel so much that I really want to see it being lived out in the lives of believers. This leads me to occasionally find myself yelling at the saints to get back on defense—confident that this team can perform far better than we currently are. I suspect this book contains chapters of both kinds—those that reflect on the glory of the Gospel and creation, and those that concentrate on what we have been doing wrong and why we need to get our head in the game. It is my hope that with all of them put together you will be encouraged in Christ. It is my hope that there is such a thing as a missionary cheerleader after all.

Your understanding of your identity affects everything in your life. Looking back on my life, I can remember various times of temptation when I was being held back from foolishness not by wisdom, not by understanding, not by insight, and not by spiritual strength. I was held back and protected by a sense of belonging: I knew who I was hanging on to, and I knew that I could never let go because He would never let go. I knew that if I took a path of sin, that not only would He not let go of me, but there would be nothing but misery until I was back in obedience.

I know that I have been given much in this by my circumstances, all free gifts to me: the faithfulness of others, a Bible-believing Christian community and teaching, and a faithful family. These are all things that I did nothing to deserve. God's mercy to me in all this has been abundant. I am no more responsible for this clarity of purpose and belonging than I am responsible for having been given hands.

Like a toddler whose legs are too short to keep up with the father who is holding his hand, I have not toddled through my life with overwhelming clarity and determination and sense of self. I have simply known that the force that was compelling me forward and taking me somewhere, keeping me out of puddles and streets, was the hand of my loving Father. I knew Him, and I have always known and believed in my core that He knows where I am going, what I am for, who I am, and who I will be. I have always known that His intention for me is perfect, and I have always known that I am right where I belong.

His fierce grip on me is the basis of all of my confidence. That is the basis of all my belonging. He knows who I am. He knows where I belong. Nothing more than that. No great confidence in my abilities or my ideas and strategies. No great achievement of self-actualization. No life flowchart that I am managing to get through in a timely and impressive manner. Nothing but God: He mine, and I His.

When I write about knowing who you are, what you are for, what the self is and isn't, and why it matters, I am writing in the abstract for the most part; but I am also writing about something that I know personally. I want you to understand that what I have, you have. What I know, you can know. He who holds me holds you. I'm not claiming that a life lived with a full sense of Christian identity is a sinless life—not by a long shot. I have told you I have always known who I am, and I can also tell you (just between us) that I have always been a sinner. This side of the grave there will never be perfection. But there can be great joy. And hope. And honesty. And laughter. And purpose. And delight.

My hope in writing this book has been to try to give others a little of what was given so freely to me. I have always been surrounded by

Christians who understood Christian identity somewhere down in their bones, and their understanding of their own purpose shaped how I learned to look to God for mine. If I can put into words the lessons I have felt, or seen, or witnessed, or struggled through myself, then by God's grace maybe you will see a way of living confidently in Christ.

If you are already secure in your identity, then maybe these things will just put words to what you already know, and perhaps encourage you to see the struggle in others, and to think of new ways to offer a lifeline. But if you have not been around Christians who are confident in their belonging, sincere in their faith, honest about their sin, and joyful in their outlook, then I want to tell you about it—because it is a glorious thing! And it belongs to you.

2

FOOLISHNESS

THE HUMAN STRUGGLE WITH IDENTITY is so pervasive that it is commonplace to hear people say things like, "I don't even know who I am anymore." This is not exclusive to unbelievers: it is also common among Christians. We have novels, stories, movies, and advertising campaigns about people who go on quests to find themselves—sometimes literal journeys, sometimes only spiritual or philosophical ones. That lost-self cry of "Who am I?" is the cry of a person who suddenly realizes that the philosophy he has been following around in the grocery store isn't his mother after all.

Our modern society has been following wrong philosophies around for generations. We have wandered so far that we need a map to find our way home. Many of us would not recognize a Christian philosophy of identity if we ran into it in the street. We are so muddled about the self and the purpose of humanity that we no longer even know where to begin. We can wander hopelessly through life like so many people do, trying out one new technique after another to try to make ourselves feel better, or we can deal with our confusion (whatever it takes) and be living and acting in the confidence of our salvation and the joy of our Lord.

Paul says in Colossians, "Now this I say lest anyone should deceive you with persuasive words" (2:4). And then a minute later "Beware lest anyone cheat you through philosophy and empty deceit" (2:8).

Worldly philosophies have fundamentally and tragically affected our modern culture. While we will be looking at some of that godless philosophical influence, I want to make clear that philosophy is not bad in itself. This book is in many ways an exercise in philosophy. The thing that Paul warns us about is not philosophy but deception. We can lose track of our fundamental beliefs through persuasive words. Empty, vain philosophies can and will cheat us of real understanding. The problem is not that we discuss ultimate things (obviously), but that we lie about them, or listen to lies. There is no gentle way of saying that the Christian world today has largely been deceived. We have listened to lies. We are entangled (though we are believers) in the consequences of unbelief. In some cases, we believe that a simple, "I believe in God" or even a vague God reference will erase all the ill effects of a deceitful philosophy. Christians must learn to look beyond the surface and evaluate the belief at its core.

The worldly philosophers and thinkers have always been something like the high-fashion designers who live in a sort of alternative reality. They make unbelievably stupid outfits for unbelievably tall and harsh looking people with show-poodle hair, wearing cinder-block shoes and pants made out of an inner tube. They do all this while praising each other as stunning and innovative and talented and surprising, taking pictures of everything and putting enormous price tags on it all. Meanwhile, most of the normal world would laugh at what they are doing. But what they are doing, however foolish it may be, is actually driving what we will all be doing next year. What looks will be in? What is every purveyor of clothes trying to channel from that groundbreaking show? That's what we all end up buying. If not this year, in a few more (once it is all on sale and we have gotten used to seeing it around). It is just the way the fashion industry works.

In the same way, regular honest people buy unbelievably foolish philosophy, but they buy it toned down and in the clearance bins. That is why we don't recognize it right away for the monstrosity it is. We buy into it through movies and shows and emotional stories about people who want to die now rather than struggle with a long illness. Isn't it the compassionate thing to support their suicide? Shouldn't we want a family to be able to put someone out of their misery? Isn't it really hateful to disagree with someone, to suggest that they are on the wrong path? We are told over and over that we should simply follow our own hearts and let others do the same. We keep bringing these things home with us and letting them grow on us. We see other professing Christians wearing them and assume that makes it okay. But if these beliefs are founded on the assumption that there is no God, what business should we have with them?

When I was in high school, I was visiting an aunt and uncle out of town and went in a beautiful new store. It was an old safari brand making a comeback. There were huge black and white photos of ships on the wall and the clothes were very classic. I bought a few things—notably a baseball cap with the name "Abercrombie and Fitch" on it. I frequently wore the things I had bought there until the catalog came in the mail. The first lines in that catalog were this: "Let's face it. We are all just looking for someone to sleep with over spring break." The article went on to explain how it was more than a clothing company—it was a lifestyle magazine, and the pages beyond this indecency were full of indecent photos. I was horrified—I had been wearing, in large print across my forehead, the name of a brand that clearly did not represent my beliefs or desires.

So it is with much of our understanding of the self. We picked it up sometime when it didn't seem bad at all. If we could just see the belief systems we are buying into spelled out in plain writing in the catalog or on the philosophical runway (so to speak), it might shock us. This is not the clothing of our people, and these are not the words we should want on our foreheads.

Unbelieving philosophies of the self begin with the assumption that there is no Father God. Then they try to make sense out of the undeniable complexity of mankind and human value. You can see right off the bat (assuming that you are a Christian) that in this way the philosophical world has nothing to offer you and much to take from you. They want to take away all meaning that you derive from God and give you a new meaning without Him.

Your premise of life is the presence of a Father Creator God, and their premise is His absence or irrelevance. Your premise is a meaning derived from Him, and theirs is mean-inglessness derived from the absence of Him. If this was as simple as a multiple-choice question about whether or not God exists, I believe Christians would pass the test with excellence. But it is not that simple. We are well past that first question, living in a society that has been assuming there is no God for a long time. As Christians, we have found ourselves knee deep in the practical consequences of wrong an-swers to the most basic questions—and often this is without having understood what the question was in the first place.

This is why I say that many Christians today do not realize that what they are struggling with on a day-to-day basis is actually, at its core, a philosophical problem. The world often uses philosophy as a substitute for religion. This is why Paul is warning us that we might be cheated of something. We might be cheated out of an understanding of our purpose and the value of life if we listen to their smooth words. We might accidentally end up with a whole bunch of false assumptions. Our understanding of life's deepest questions is what shapes our action on the shallower questions of life. If you were navigating a ship by the pole star, it would matter if you got confused about which star it was. When you face any obstacle or difficulty or decision, you will rely on your deeply held beliefs to help you. We return to the first beliefs, the fundamental things. In such times as this, when we have been so deceived as a culture, we need to go back and make sure that our fixed things are the right fixed things. What if we have been cheated? What if we have been deceived through vain words? I believe that we have been. But how did this happen?

3

A PHILOSOPHY STARTER

THE FIRST TIME I EVER REALLY NOTICED the philosophical problem of the self was in college. I was writing a paper on it and spent some time I will never get back reading philosophers so I could respond to them with a biblical perspective. I have not stopped seeing the problem of the self out on the streets in all of its shiny confusion since that time. It is the thing that won't stop showing up once you have become aware of it. Where I often see it is all tangled up in the regular lives of Christians, keeping them in a state of muddled confusion for no good reason.

These next few chapters may feel a little bizarre or a little heavy, a little irrelevant in your regular life, or a little impractical. But I hope you will trust me with your time long enough to hear the point. I keep thinking of Ignaz Semmelweis, that Hungarian doctor in the 1840s, who first proposed that doctors washing their hands between dealing with cadavers and delivering babies would cut down on maternal deaths. At the time, everyone laughed at his theories.

If you are not interested in philosophy naturally, you may want to laugh at my theories here. You might think philosophy is not a part of your life because you don't call it by its name. But many thousands of Christian women today are sick from the consequences of this discussion. We don't know who we are. We don't know why we matter. We don't know how to walk through our lives with purpose and meaning. We don't know how to be. We are sick because we won't consider these first things.

The problem of the self is a very old philosophical question. Who am I? What am I for? What makes me who I am in essence? Am I able to change that? Can another person

change that? Am I the same person I have always been? What is the essential me? Where is
the essential me? How do I find out? How do I
come into being?

Change is a reality in our world. When dealing with the self, how do we know we have one
essence, one self through time, per person? Are
you the same person (in essence) as you were
as a child? What if you go through some major
change? Can your identity be taken away from
you? Can your self be lost? What is the nature
of the continuity of the self? Am I who I have
always been?

A simple example of this problem of continuity is the ancient puzzle of the ship of Theseus.
The ship sails out from port on a long journey.
Throughout the journey it needs to stop in various places for repairs. Because the journey is
so long, by the time the ship comes back home,
every single part of it has been replaced. Is it
the same ship that left port?

Now, assuming that you answered yes because it has some kind of continuity of identity
going for it, imagine that someone was sailing
along behind it the whole time, collecting every
discarded piece of the old ship and rebuilding
it. So in the end one ship is the original ship and

one is the new one. Which one is the real ship of Theseus?

While it might not seem like the worst trouble if we don't know the answer to this, it is a very real trouble when we apply the problem to humans. Your body, while not a ship exactly, is made up of component parts. Those parts (cells) routinely replace themselves. Your body is in a constant state of discarding itself and making a new self. What does that mean for your identity? Is your essential self in all the parts of your body, or just in one super important place? Is it able to be lost? Is it really possible that when you are fifty, you could look back on a picture of yourself at eight and be looking at a different person entirely? Most of your cells are not the same as they were then. Think of someone who goes through a radical weight loss journey and they look like a completely different person, they act like a completely different person, and they feel like a completely different person. They have new likes and new habits and completely different ways of being. Are they actually a new person?

One of the common ideas that is sometimes advanced is that your true identity is in your memories. This theory argues that memories are a feature of what someone might call "psychological continuity." In the instance of radical weight loss, according to this theory, the memory is what ties the person together. The skinny, active person has memories of being the heavy, tired person, so we can assume they are the same person. Even as a very old person, you could have the memories of being a child, which in some way proves it was you who was that child.

And yet, there remains a major problem with this. We know that human memories fail us. Is an elderly person with memory loss no longer herself? Was the memory the only thing that bound her to her younger self? What if you sustained a head injury and lost a chunk of your life memories? Is it no longer you who lived through those things? Are you no longer the mother of your children or the wife of your husband? Of course you are. Your memory or knowledge of what has happened to you is not the fundamental thing that ties your essential self to your body. There must be more here. We shouldn't be able to lose our essential self, misplacing it like a stack of papers waiting to be filed.

I hope you can see how practically relevant these questions are. If you believe that true

human identity (and consequently human value and dignity) are only present in the active
mind (memory), then there is no human value,
identity, or dignity in a person who has sustained a sudden brain injury that resulted in
brain damage. It isn't a theoretical question at
all. If you think they are no longer a person,
then you would believe it is fine to stop feed-
ing them and to let them die at your hands.
In some ways I think "identity" is the world's
shorthand for "meaning." And if the meaning
has gone out of a person, there is no reason to
bother with them anymore.

Christian answer

This is our simple answer to all of this: we
believe that we were made with a soul. We believe that our physical bodies are not the whole
story. We have an identity that is spoken by
God, sustained by God, and even our physical
body replaces itself according to God's design.
At the end of the day we aren't merely mortal,
but eternal beings. The Christian concept of
the soul makes most of these questions irrelevant. The soul is not located in one place in
your body. You may get a leg amputated, but
your soul stays with you. You sustain a brain injury, but your soul is not lost. You start with one
soul, and it stays with you all the way until you

die, and even then your soul goes on living. The essential you will never die—it is eternal.

When you remove the role of the active Creator from the discussion, you are left with a bunch of human component parts that have no direction and make no sense. Everyone knows that something much bigger is going on here, but the worldly philosophers will act like fools while trying to avoid God and His image in His creation.

Traditionally, philosophy has fallen back on the idea that it is really our brains (rational thought) that make us people. We hold on to the brain idea and rational thought or memories as the origin of the self for a few reasons.

First, our brains are the only difference we see between ourselves and the animals. Memories, communication, civilization—these are all things that are a result of our brains in some way. Rene Descartes (pronounced *day-CART*) famously wrote "*Cogito ergo sum*" ("I think, therefore I am") and set the stage for much of our understanding of the mind as the most important part of a human. It seems that the idea of the brain being the origin of our personhood is easy and natural to many people. After all, it is our thought life that makes us

different from the animals. It also appeals because we think we have control over our rational thought. If we can calmly think up the existence of ourselves, then surely we could think
our way into new selves and new ways of being.

Unfortunately, this assumption also draws
lines right through the middle of humanity. If
we exist because of our thoughts, then we cannot exist without them. There are adults who
lose their rational thought. What about young
babies who are not rational thinkers yet? Do
you lose track of your rationality when you are
asleep? At what point in your thought life have
you risen to existence? In the womb? When you
first spoke? When you first expressed an original thought? Does it have to be a good thought
to make you exist? When we believe human
identity and value is in our thoughts—when our
very existence is tied up in those things—then
we have to believe that many people are only
formerly of value, and that people with mental
impairments are less *people* than those without.

The philosophy of the self is basically wrestling with the problem that, without a God, we
might simply be animals, but we really don't feel
like animals. Many philosophers believe that our
lives are fundamentally meaningless (because

there is no God, we are the result of an accident, etc.), and yet they still have an enormous need for meaning. We search for it; we long for it. We are hungry for meaning and our rational thoughts are not enough to satisfy us.

Now, most Christians are not struggling with the philosophical problems themselves. But we must provide the right answers to the questions that the world has already answered wrongly. They aren't asking us for answers—they are assuming their own bad answers, and in many cases leading us along with them. It is easy to miss what is being assumed. Christians are often ill at ease with questions regarding assisted suicide or any serious discussion about human value (such as abortion). We don't know exactly where the whole thing went wrong. Why is this so difficult? Why don't we feel confident about this? I believe it is because we desperately need to go back and evaluate all those first questions.

4

SORTING OUT SARTRE

"BEWARE LEST ANYONE CHEAT YOU through philosophy and empty deceit, according to the tradition of men, according to the basic principles of the world, and not according to Christ" (Col. 2:8).

Nihilism (the belief that all of existence is devoid of meaning and that nothing really matters anyway) should be easy for a Christian to recognize. This is the really bad counterfeit money that very few people who are looking for real meaning will fall for. Friedrich Nietzsche (pronounced NEE-*chuh*) is the best-known philosopher who is associated with nihilism, but many different philosophers have dabbled to different sorrowful depths in this particular mud pit. There is a profound hopelessness to it. As Christians, we ought to know well that we have hope. When nihilism creeps into the view of self, what we will see is usually drug addiction, crime, hopeless despair, self-hatred and loathing, self-mutilation, and just dead sorrow.

Nihilism is still a heavy influence in our world today, but this is a class of philosophical struggle that Christians recognize usually as the big E on the eye chart of spiritual hunger. We know that someone in this case needs Christ. They need to know that they have value. They need to know that Jesus loves them. They need to know there is help and hope, and a future with meaning. This is something that Christians are traditionally quite well equipped for. You don't have hope, you say? *I have that!* No one cares about you? *Yes! Jesus does!* You feel a great gnawing void in your life? *I know the answer!* Nihilistic expressions are to Christianity like a great lobbing softball to a well-positioned batter. It is hard to miss.

I do not think that nihilism has deceived many true Christians. In order to get us off our

guard it needs to be much closer to our experience of reality, or at least a little bit attractive.

Existentialism is related to nihilism, but we
don't recognize it because it is all dressed up
in human action. It appeals to us because it
majors on what we might make of ourselves.
Existentialism is a belief that has been accepted
by many philosophers, but most famously Jean-
Paul Sartre. Sartre gave existentialism this accessible definition: *Existence precedes Essence.*

> What do we mean by saying that existence
> precedes essence? We mean that man first of
> all exists, encounters himself, surges up in the
> world—and defines himself afterwards. If man as
> the existentialist conceives him is not definable,
> it is because to begin with he is nothing. He will
> not be anything until later, and then he will be
> what he makes of himself.[1]

The idea here is that you don't mean anything, objectively. You exist as a person before
you mean anything. Existence comes before
you have any essence (which is the value of

1. "Existentialism is a Humanism," trans. Philip Mairet, in *Existentialism from Dostoevsky to Sartre, Revised and Expand-
ed Edition*, ed. Walter Kaufmann (1956; New York: Penguin
Group, 1975), 360.

life) at all. Essence is something that only happens through your own action. You only "mean"
anything, you only develop an *essence*, through
your own exertion. You make your own meaning. You must take responsibility—and your action drives your meaning.

Sartre did not see his teaching as hopeless,
but rather as the only means for any hope.
Having discarded the idea of God the Father, he
still wanted to inspire men to action. He taught
that you were free to be anything if only you
could make yourself that through action. And
Sartre's counterfeit ideas about the purpose of
life and the way we should approach the idea
of ourselves are still in broad circulation today.
I saw a motivational poster recently that said
something like this: "You are the pen, the ink,
and the poem." This kind of thing has its origins
in the existential movement. *You are what you
make yourself, your story is yours to create, and
what you are can only exist through your action.*

Sartre concluded his famous lecture on existentialism and humanism with this statement
(emphasis mine):

Existentialism is nothing else but an attempt
to draw the full conclusions from a *consistently*

atheistic position. Its intention is not in the least that of plunging men into despair. And if by despair one means as the Christians do—any attitude of unbelief, the despair of the existentialists is something different. Existentialism is not atheist in the sense that it would exhaust itself in demonstrations of the non-existence of God. It declares, rather, that even if God existed that would make no difference from its point of view. Not that we believe God does exist, but we think that the real problem is not that of His existence; *what man needs is to find himself again and to understand that nothing can save him from himself,* not even a valid proof of the existence of God. In this sense existentialism is optimistic.[2]

While many philosophers have put different angles and nuances on existentialism, what they all have in common is this idea that existence precedes essence: the importance of you is entirely up to you. The real meaning in your life is only what you make it. But as you can see from the quote above, this belief system specifically rejects God the Father. Even if He is real, Sartre says, He has nothing to do with all of this that's around us. In the same lecture

2. "Existentialism is a Humanism," 369.

he continues, "But if I have excluded God the Father, there must be somebody to invent values." In other words, without God the Father it is every man to himself.

When put this way, I hope every Christian would reject existentialism, because it is clearly built on the absence of objective meaning, absence of God the Father, and absence of any intention or purpose for humanity that exists outside of each one of us individually. Sartre is frankly admitting that he is inventing values out of his own private brain. For his own private purposes. To make himself what he wants. To inspire us all to be whatever we want. The one truly remarkable thing about this is that he managed to become very influential!

Existentialist thinking has pervaded our culture. *You can be whatever you want to be. If you set your mind to it, you can be it. You are the only one who can decide what you are.* This is the philosophy of Disney movies, spoon-fed to our children from toddlerhood. We love the idea that we are made with the power of our own will. *You are a powerful woman if you want to be a powerful woman. Decide what you want to be, and you are on your way to being it. Believe that you are beautiful, and you will be beautiful.*

These are all very commonplace admonitions, and what we need to remember is that they find their origins in this particular godless philosophy. These are Sartre's ideas, no longer on the runway, but in the clearance bins of the big box store being purchased everywhere by women who feel needy.

In the assumed absence of God the Father, Sartre stepped up to tell us all how to be—what we are for, how to go about becoming more, etc. He stood in for God the Father for us and explained *us* to us. And we listened.

What kind of a person have we given this authority to? There is no denying that Jean-Paul Sartre and Simone de Beauvoir were a radically influential couple. You will have seen black and white photos of the cafe life in Paris in the early 20th century—men and women in suits, enjoying a glamorous intellectual life. Jazz bars and the theater, coffee and cigarettes—an aura of intelligence hanging around them as they wrestle with the big issues of life. These two were the heart and soul of this movement, as they lived their existentialist philosophy out. They thought there was no objective meaning behind their lives, no set purpose for it. What they became was entirely up to their own actions.

Simone became a prominent feminist, and author of *The Second Sex*. The couple had met at school in 1929 and were immediately drawn to each other. She was a well-known intellect, and generally considered a beauty. They determined to never marry, rejecting such a bourgeois tradition, and claimed to be entering into a new kind of transparent life. They never lived together as a couple, but they promised to tell each other everything, including their other sexual encounters. To everyone watching, it appeared to be working for them. They became more famous and more successful even as their bizarre relationship became more known (revealed to the public in their own writing).

Although Sartre was a short (five-foot) and wall-eyed man, his one real strength being his words, he managed to seduce many women. He claimed to be devoted to transparency, but he lied constantly to these women in all of the tropes of romance: "I cannot live without you," and "You are my world." He lied to them to keep them happy as his mistresses. His letters tell the stories unabashedly and frankly. He was not hiding the fact that he lied his way into and through these things. Sartre had one bad trip on mescaline that left him thinking he

SORTING OUT SARTRE   35

was being followed by crabs (literally) for years. Medical uppers were common at the time, and where most people might take half of a tablet, Sartre would chew up four and write frantically for hours.

Simone got involved with many men and also some young teenage girls, most of them students of hers. In some cases, she handed them off to Sartre. The couple spent much time developing these relationships with girls, often making them financially dependent on them first. Jean-Paul and Simone paid their rent and their tuition to acting schools or painting lessons. They gathered up girls who were adrift, needy orphans, or immigrants, and offered them shelter and work, a sort of perverse, makeshift family for the philosophically inclined.

The two of them rejected the "hypocrisy" of the old style. But this new way of living turned out to allow for even greater hypocrisy. Few things were less honest and transparent than their private lives. When Sartre died, his letters to Simone were edited and published. When she died, the unedited collection of letters was released. What those letters show the public (beyond much promiscuity) is what a sad, long, and hypocritical time it all was. Many of the people involved with them were still living when these letters were published—a shocking and embarrassing way to see what they had really thought of you all along.

These letters show a side of their lives that was not visible to the public at the time. They tore women apart, dissecting their "lovers" to each other in horrible, mean-hearted detail. When Sartre finally got a young girl named Wanda into bed with him (after two years of pursuing her constantly), he immediately wrote to Simone that he had left her in bed, "all pure and tragic, declaring herself tired and having hated me for a good forty-five minutes."

While Simone denied sleeping with women in interviews during her lifetime, her letters tell a different story as she recounts every detail to Sartre. They were far from the free and easy pair the world thought them to be. Instead, they lived a sexually debauched life with plot points that would probably have landed them in prison today.

To readers of their letters it is clear that Simone was consumed with a tragic jealousy, and Sartre was consumed with himself. She often begged him to lie to the other women he was with and spend a week with her at some secret place before his current mistress would know he was in town. Her jealousy was not a secret between them, but they both viewed it as a weakness.

They referred to their young women as their "family," playing up the incestuous nuances. Sartre had a brief affair with a girl named Arlette Elkaim, and then adopted her as his daughter in 1965. She is the heir to his estate. Simone also adopted a daughter, Sylvie Le Bon. The two met in 1960 when Sylvie was 17 and Simone 57. In her words they had a relationship that was "carnal but not sexual." She is the heir to Simone's estate.

Sartre was wildly popular in his time. He was a successful playwright (even though his plays seemed mostly to be a way to keep his mistresses busy), he loved the nightlife, he wrote songs, he gave lectures, he lived an intellectual life in Paris cafes, and he did it all as though he was free from convention. France has always loved philosophers, and he and Simone were considered two of the greatest minds of the twentieth century. Their unique relationship settled them as fascinating people—people who were living differently and, apparently, free from the things that tie down regular people.

They managed to keep the public charade up for their whole lives—probably because they wanted to believe it as badly as everyone else. When they openly doubted their choices to each other, they kept one another in line. They told each other to not feel guilty—that this was the way to really live. Many people believed they were actually succeeding in doing what they said could be done. Now that the whole story can be seen, many people claim that their horrible lifestyle was not really related to the philosophy they taught—because we still want to believe that it might be possible.

Sartre explains his counsel to a young man during the war who was feeling conflicted about avenging his brother or staying with his mother. This was the final statement Sartre gave him—a perfect summary of his counsel for everyone for all of life: "You are free, therefore choose, that is to say, invent. No rule of general morality can show you what you ought to do: no signs are vouchsafed in this world."[3]

When Sartre died in 1980, around fifty thousand mourners flooded the streets of Paris to follow his funeral procession. I imagine much could be said about what brought the world to readiness to receive the teaching of such a debauched and selfish man with very little to

3. "Existentialism is a Humanism," 356.

recommend him. It seems that the two great wars left his nation (and the world) vulnerable. I believe it was a gospel moment—a moment when people needed meaning and understanding about how they fit in. They needed to know what to do, and Sartre gave them the answer without God: *Do whatever you want!* He taught people not to see themselves as part of any other story, but rather to write their own story without reference to anything else. Given the painful war experience that France had just been through (not just the loss of life and fighting but having lost Paris to the Nazis for a time), many people were troubled by their social context. It was a difficult time, and there was much to appeal to people in the ideas of existentialism. Forget about duty, honor, glory, and faithfulness. What did they achieve anyway besides tragedy? Make up your own values. Be whoever you want to be. Sartre believed that this was a big responsibility and not the easy path. In other words, he was calling people to the great "moral duty" of doing whatever you want.

It is truly tragic that this man is the origin of most of our cultural ideas about who we are and what we are for. While we might find it easy to reject Sartre himself (with all of his womanizing and lying), it will take a careful evaluation of our cultural assumptions to reject the damage that he has done. Remember that we are living downstream of so many people who have done what he told them to do and built their ideas of life on his ideas. This is not the kind of thing that can be quickly undone.

If you are setting out to remodel a home that has rotten floorboards, one of the first steps must be an evaluation of the extent of the damage. What needs to be torn out? That is the first question for us to consider. Later we will deal with what to put in instead.

5

THE PINNACLE
THAT ISN'T

ANOTHER IMPORTANT MAN IN THE history of how we view the self is Abraham Maslow. He was an atheist psychologist who built his very famous theory of the hierarchy of needs on the premises of humanism and existentialism. That famous triangle is all about our drive toward the great pinnacle of life as a human—what is commonly called self-actualization.

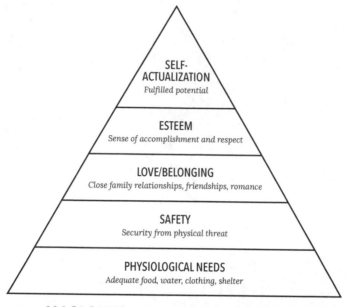

MASLOW'S HIERARCHY OF NEEDS

The idea behind this was that as humans are able to secure each level of need, they are then equipped to pursue the next one.

The baseline need is just physiological: sleep, food, shelter, oxygen, etc. This is the level of need that simply keeps us alive. Once a man has established this level of need fulfillment, then he can go on to the next tier of needs—safety.

Safety needs would be reflected in physical security, protection, and stability. A person at this level of need fulfillment would want a safe place to live, a secure job, might be planning for retirement, etc. Once we have fulfilled this level of need, we can move on to the next tier, which is about our social life.

The idea is that once your basic needs are met, and you are safe and feel secure, then you can reach out and make friends. You can start to serve in your church or community, get married, and have children. At this phase in the journey toward self-actualization you want to have a sense of belonging and social community.

Once you have reached this level of need fulfillment, you can press on to some of the more elite levels of human experience, esteem needs. This is both the self-esteem we hear so much about and also the esteem of others. A person who has achieved this level and is feeling a sense of belonging and security and stability is now free to simply add on to their own accomplishments. A person seeking to fill this level of need would be hotly pursuing her career, looking for promotions. She might be contending for recognition and advancement, or maybe just really devoted to self-improvement in hobbies and interests. This level of need is often seen in the gym—striving for esteem in any area that seems likely to give back. This phase of the need pyramid is all about feeling capable and competent and confident, being secure, and having a solid sense of self-worth.

Now at last, if you have made it through all these need hurdles, you can finally approach the ultimate in human fulfillment, the holy grail of self-actualization.

This is essentially the tiny tip-top of human experience. The ultimate moment where you are able to see mankind as basically good. It is here that you know fully who you are, you are at ease in the world and know your place in it.

Maslow was influenced by Sigmund Freud, who had made himself famous through psychoanalysis, studying the troubled human mind. Freud studied the mind from the direction of things that go wrong, and Maslow sought to fill out the ideas surrounding how to grow into a complete human in the right way. Specifically, Maslow was trying to understand the nature of human motivation.

Maslow is considered the father of humanistic psychology. This means that while he assumed the premises of existentialism, he went about his business of trying to help people develop themselves into the kind of people who can experience life fully. As the father of humanist psychology, he is also the source of much of the counsel, life coaching, and self-help our world has received. He saw a future of self-actualized people who knew that man is basically good, understood their place in the world, and saw their own value and worth. It was an optimistic way of looking at the growth of the human self because, no matter how bad things look, there is always this idea that you might still be growing into a successful, fully actualized human, able to move on to the next level.

Maslow's hierarchy of needs is still in use in college counseling and is often still assumed by many people to be an accurate representation of the growth of the human person, a description of how a complete self comes about. While Maslow did not believe that many humans would reach self-actualization, of course most people would like to. Self-actualization is generally seen as the goal, coming to terms with yourself and the world, and being at ease in it.

There are so many examples of the way that this thought process has entered itself into the mainstream. How many people assume that when we are searching for a spouse, we should be looking for someone who will help us become our best selves? This is the kind of winsome advice that is given in a million chick flicks and a million magazine articles. It assumes the idea that when you are entering into relationships you are filling one of your own needs. You have a stair-step need on your way to your next self-manifesting opportunity, and your spouse and your children, your neighborhood, and your church community are part of your need fulfillment. When you are volunteering in your community, you are doing so to become your best self. But is this the biblical idea? Do we marry and have children to better meet our own needs? The answer is a resounding "No, we don't!" What could go wrong here, other than everything?

Another example is the idea that your career, in order to be serving your self-actualizing needs, must be equipping your esteem needs. Of course if you are a little less mature as an individual, then all your career would have to fulfill would be the need of security. But if you are wanting to mature fully as a person, then your career must fill your need for esteem. You should be feeling increasingly significant. You should be having more opportunities to become important and be confident. At least this should be happening if you are still heading toward self-actualization. A career becomes a stepping stone toward being your best self.

What about those who do not have careers, as such? What about a woman who decides to stay at home with the children? You now know enough to see why our society thinks that is a choice to be a lesser human with inferior motivation and goals. If you decide not to work on the esteem level of the need hierarchy, then you are deciding never to move past it into full-on Best-Selfing. It is seen as a failure in motivation. But biblically speaking, is it? Again, the answer is a loud *no*. This is overtly anti-biblical teaching

The final goal of the hierarchy of needs is the desire for man to feel "right" in the world. This is the goal that so many are working toward, and why so many are discarding the relationships and careers and obligations that they see as holding them back, as they press on, trying to become the best version of themselves that they can be, looking for the job that is so fulfilling that it doesn't feel like work anymore.

But this is not a gospel-based approach to life. Christians agree that man is not right in the world, and we agree that something must be done to get us right. But that is the starting point of the Christian faith and not the end destination. We need to be put right with God. We start there—at being made right with God at the cross of Jesus Christ. Things get upended for the Christian at the outset, at conversion. From that point we work out our new life in Christ. We work out our salvation. We lay down our own interests and see others as more important. We work to give to others rather than consume others on our way to our new, completed selves. In Christianity, the self is always a tool and never a destination.

Maslow took the kinds of beliefs that Sartre held and overlaid it with this mythical idea of how any human could become someone admirable. We could simply check off these boxes and be on our way to the top. Because Maslow was more optimistic and gave everyone handles on the road to self-actualization, his ideas took off. They were well received, and he himself was much admired. His contributions to humanistic psychology are remembered fondly. But he didn't know God, and that means on a fundamental level he could not know man. God doesn't give us the Maslow kind of roadmap.

In fact, Matthew 6:31–33 says something quite the opposite: "Therefore do not worry, saying, 'What shall we eat?' or 'What shall we drink?' or

'What shall we wear?' For after all these things the Gentiles seek. For your heavenly Father knows that you need all these things. But seek first the kingdom of God and His righteousness, and all these things shall be added to you."

Seek first the kingdom of God and His righteousness. Everything else—food, clothing, and drink—will be handled by your heavenly Father when you first seek Him.

I hope you can see how many ways this kind of worldly thinking has slipped into our lives. It has crept into Christian counseling. It has crept into our marriages and families, and it has crept into our whole idea of humanity. But when we look at it in the pure light of day, we can see that it is nothing but the rot of unbelief, and we should not be building our lives on it.

6

THE NARRATIVE OF YOU

IT ISN'T LIKELY THAT YOU WILL FIND yourself having a philosophical or psychological discussion in line at the grocery store, but that doesn't mean that the assumptions of our confused philosophies will not be present there. Existentialism and humanistic psychology have worked their way into our cultural thought processes without most of us even knowing its name. Existentialist damage is everywhere, and more floorboards are rotted out than we want to believe. If we think that we are responsible to make ourselves through our own action, we are certainly going to try to do so. So how will we attempt to craft ourselves, and what are the results of us trying?

Common today is what we can call the narrative view of the self. It is something of a mashup of existential thought and popular psychology. It is the Sartre-Maslow hybrid: how you become what you are—and what makes you *you*. This sort of "philosophy" is at the root of self-help. It is the nitty-gritty, how-to section that comes after the theory.

We want to know what really matters in our quest for becoming us. The narrative view of self seems like the most realistic of all explanations because it views the self as a story, and we all know that we are in one. We have a beginning, a middle, and an end. We start out somewhere, and we keep adding plot points through time. We assemble those things that matter to us, and we imagine we can assemble a self that we will admire. This fits in with the concept of progression in the hierarchy of needs.

But the truth is, the reason this approach appeals to everyone is because it flatters us. We are the makers of our own essences! If we want to be outdoorsy, we shall be so! It is only a trip to Cabela's away! If we want to care a lot about charity, we need only take some action in that direction and slap it on our personal narrative like a bumper sticker on an old car. We drive through our lives pasting things onto the back windshield of our selves. Maybe we have a child, so we get a vinyl stick figure to put next to the dog. Then maybe we feel crafty, or we do some training and run a marathon, and so we add a couple more. It's all in pursuit of that identity of the self that we think we are creating. We keep on going like that, trying to assemble decals and bumper stickers into a coherent story about a character we like, going somewhere we like, and doing things we like. I recently heard an ad on Spotify encouraging me to purchase a premium account because my life deserves a nonstop, uninterrupted playlist to help me be the person I want to be.

Of course it is true that we choose various things and don't choose others, and that reveals something about us. What you devote your time to will end up shaping you in some way. The trouble is when a whole society believes that this is the essence, the formulation, the very heart of the self. Your degree. Your job. Your car. Your hobbies. What you make time for.

What you like. Wine. Dogs. Fashion. What you look like on Instagram. Your tiny little byline on social media—a biography to be proud of! *Artsy, loves coffee and Jesus.* What is the soundtrack to your life story? We think we are making ourselves from scratch, and we love to admire our work.

Over time we change; something that was critically important we no longer view as essential. Maybe we are even embarrassed by it. We want to put a new sticker over the old one on our life and change our essence. We want to reinvent ourselves through the power of our own will and our own actions. If we are going to be the story, then we think we are certainly going to be the author, too.

Now, this may all seem casual and cheerful and not at all a big deal. Handcrafting your self like a scrapbooking project sounds fun and creative, so it may surprise you that there are enormous ethical problems with this idea and these assumptions. It may seem pretty fine and harmless as long as we are talking about zero-conflict situations. But in real life that is never what we are talking about.

When we get started with the wrong assumptions, we will certainly not be equipped to find our way out. Let's look at a couple of ways this assumption plays out in society. Note that these are some of the big-ticket confusions of our time. It isn't like I am imagining this concern or getting alarmist. Also notice that some of these concerns are similar to the questions we brought up when discussing Descartes.

First of all, if our essence is what gives us value as people, and our essence is our own hand-crafted story, what is the value of people who do not have the ability or opportunity to be whatever they want to be, like a handicapped or dependent person? Does their situation make them of less value? Our society is saying yes, that makes you less of a person. This is where Christians lose all kinds of ground on issues like euthanasia or assisted suicide. If someone wants to die, who are we to argue with them? If someone cannot make their own decisions about their life, what possible value could that life have? If it is the will and action of the individual that makes us what we are, how could someone without a will or the ability for action matter as a human? Remember that Sartre taught us that our existence comes before our essence. Without action we have no essence, and this means that mere existence does not imply the presence of a true self.

This same vein of reasoning affects how we deal with privilege. If you are born in a third-world country with no opportunity or freedom to pamper yourself (like we do), are you less of a person? We bring this concern into our modern arguments about privilege because we see the problem with our idea of the self, but we do not know how to fix it. If you believe that some people actually have a head start, not just in status and careers and schooling, but in actual *personhood*, what a horrible unfairness it would be. And what would that mean for us? When you remove the Creator God from the story, you have removed the image of God (our true human value). If there is no Creator, then our situation can actually remove our personhood from us. Were people who lived in far more difficult times than ours less human than we are? If we think back to Maslow's hierarchy of needs, we will find that some people are never able to move past those initial steps of simple physiological needs and security and safety. What if your situation never allows for that? Have you really been kept from your own personhood? Your own self? Do you think these ideas have consequences in our time? People are looking for their own human value in a society that they believe is denying them the opportunity.

Second, how do we evaluate who matters more when there is a clash of interests? What if a young woman (who is only beginning to create her own identity) becomes accidentally pregnant? What if she does not want to be a mother? What if, in the creation of her own self, the creation of another person is something she would like to edit out? This is the foundational desire of abortion rights. This is the belief that a woman should be free to decide for herself what will make it into her story. This is why birth control has always been an integral part of the feminist agenda. If the whole idea is to choose your own destiny and make your own self, you can see how a woman's fertility does actually make her less of a person by removing some of her options on the path toward self-actualization.

If your essence is in your choices, anything that takes away your own free will and choices is obviously the enemy. A woman does not want any of these literary tropes (like motherhood) to be forced on her, because that would indicate a level of obedience to something outside herself. Remember that she is writing her own story—she is in charge of her own destiny! No one may insert things of such importance without her permission, and it certainly may not come to fruition in her life without her actively choosing to let it do so. In this context, it makes sense that feminists would see abortion as the only means to get womankind on the same level of freedom as men.

This is why, in recent years, the abortion movement has become more and more honest about what is happening without being deterred from the mission. They know it is murder (as it is now perfectly clear that a life is being taken), and they don't care. They are no longer trying to hide what is happening, because they believe that, even when the facts are all presented, it is still fine for the woman to choose to end the life of another (dependent) human being. They believe it is acceptable for a woman to write sex into her life and simply edit out the consequences. In fact, it's more than a belief: she *must* have that freedom if she is going to be the author of her self. Because the infant is only existence as of now, and not any essence (having never exercised its will or done anything), it cannot be compared to its mother. There is

no equity of value. While they say it is only a fe-
tus, only a blob of cells, only nothing—what they
mean is that it is not yet a person because it is
not yet writing its own story. It should come as
no surprise that this logic is growing to cover
the category of young infants, the old and frail,
the disabled, and the mentally unwell.

I say these things make sense because they
flow naturally from the first assumption—which
is that we create our own essences through our
own actions. We develop the self intentionally through time (as its creators). As Christians
we cannot abide by those first assumptions. We
do not self-create. We do not have that kind of
creative power.

7

A CHAPTER OF HATE

ALL THIS CONFUSION AROUND THE self has affected society in the broad category of "identity issues." When individuals are making choices and writing their own narrative (creating themselves from nothing, as it were) they may make choices that push the boundaries of our culture.

A large percentage of them certainly will try. They want to believe they are creating themselves, not just going along with old cultural norms. The more important "self-creation" is to people, the more they will need to make specifically counter-cultural decisions just to prove themselves to themselves.

Men might decide to have green hair, tattoos of monkeys on their faces, implant horns or huge breasts, or even castrate themselves and take hormones because they have decided that they are no longer men and will now be women. They believe they are free to say whatever they want about themselves, to do whatever accords with their own will, and to be whoever it was that they wanted to be. This has been established as a right to personal expression and is essentially a right to person-making.

Today, this is a far more protected right than the right to life. What we Christians need to see is that this is completely consistent with the existential viewpoint. We are having this trouble because we believed that lie.

Christians believe that the value of life begins at conception because that is when God creates a unique human life. A unique human life has unique human value. It does not need to *do* anything to have value. The value is found in what God did by creating it. Sartre believed that you were nothing until you did something; we believe you are nothing until God does something.

For those in the grip of an existential world-view, they believe the thing that deserves protection is the true essence of a self, and that begins when a person starts making decisions for himself. They believe that a life of value begins when an individual begins to tell his own story by acting on his own desires. This is why a very liberal culture does not mind the idea of even young children going through gender changes, having abortions, or experimenting sexually. To them this is the fundamental right to life, and that is something they want protected no matter what.

Just as Christians honor pregnancy in its earliest stages because God gives value to life, modern day "human rights" advocates honor even the beginnings of self-expression because they believe that gives value to life. They honor the concept of an independent self-expression that rebels against God and/or society because they believe that is the genesis of a true human. It doesn't matter if such an effort is weak, lame, or in no way original, because to them it has the value of life. It represents everything they care about.

We value personhood similarly, but our valuations are built on a completely different foundation. Who you believe does the creating makes all the difference. Which creator do we honor?

Many Christian women have wondered why their choices to be married and to nurture children are seen by feminists as anti-woman. If the feminists are so big on women making choices for themselves, then it seems like they ought to support women who make a choice to nurture children.

However, the more these people believe that the only true living is done in defiance of God and tradition, the more natural it seems to them to despise people who are living in clear accordance with their created purposes. They believe making your own values is an essential part of finding your essence. This is why "choice" has always been an integral part of the abortion rhetoric. They don't really mean the choice between life or death; they mean a choice between having to do what God created you to do or getting to create yourself in defiance of Him. "Choice" is just a more positive word than "rebellion." Obviously, through the years many more things have influenced women, and there is much water under that historical bridge. But fundamentally, at its heart, the abortion movement is simply a bunch of women yelling at God, "You can't make me! I will decide who I am!"

Imagine for a moment that you have grown up in this way of thinking. Imagine you have always believed that it was up to you to craft yourself. You have bought into inspirational quotes such as this gem from Nathan W. Morris: "Edit your life frequently and ruthlessly. It's your masterpiece after all." You believe absolutely that you are creating a story in which you are the hero and that it is your responsibility to make this story what you want it to be. You must make yourself what you need to be because that is the only way to live fully! So, you select things that you want to be in this masterpiece. You might add an interest in houseplants. You might edit out a toxic aunt. You might add spin class, or you might edit out additional responsibilities and clutter. You are crafting the story the way you want it to be. Say that what you are trying to self-actualize is an interesting, vibrant, well-loved and fun person. In addition, say that in this self-created world you are also (either coincidentally or centrally) a lesbian, or gay, or trans, or whatever other status you may have decided to incorporate. You see the story this way, and you think it is wonderful and intriguing and fun, and it is all according to your plan for who you think you are. You intentionally wrote these things into your story, or you discovered them to be part of your identity, so you have decided to feature them.

Given all this imaginary set up, do you see why it would feel like hate if Christians did not "affirm" your story? It would feel truly spiteful because it would seem like someone had come into your story to criticize it unfairly. If you penned in all these things with a note in the margin ("and everyone loved her and was jealous of her life"), then even a quiet disagreement with your choices from others would make you (the author) into a liar.

Imagine that you are confidently writing your story assuming the genre is romantic comedy. Imagine a Christian coming in to tell you (the tone of voice is really irrelevant here) that actually this is a tragedy and the main character is about to die.

But how? How could someone else dare to make you a liar in your own story? How could the author become a liar about herself? You do get to write your own story, don't you? Isn't this what everyone has always told you? How dare anyone come along and flat-out deny your truth? How dare they say, "No, you aren't a boy, and you never will be." How dare they tell you that you may not do whatever you want to do or be whatever you want to be? How dare they come and tell you that you are not the author and that this story is wholly other than what you think you have been writing? As a trans person recently said to someone who refused to use their special pronoun, "Are you denying my existence?!"

This is not a collision of preferences or manners. This is a collision of answers to the most basic questions of life we discussed at the beginning: "Who are we? Who decides? What does it mean, and why does it matter anyway?"

If the Christian idea about identity is right, then all the self-constructed people in the world have just been building their little selves out in the thin air off the cliff edge like so many Wile E. Coyotes. The bottom isn't about to fall out from under them because it has never been there at all. There is no safety, there is no refuge, there is no security. It is understandable that all they can see in our Christian claims is hate.

But from our Christian perspective, speaking the truth is very far away from hate. The more any of us tries to cobble together the pieces of things around us—racial identity, sexual identity, hobby identity, political identity, pet owner identity, the smaller we become. In other words, the more we try to build up an identity apart from God and apart from His Word, the less truly "*us*" we become. It doesn't matter how long or thoughtful or detailed the story you are writing is. If it is written by a character in the story rather than the Author of the story, it can only ever be tiny; it will always be minuscule by comparison. You cannot, as a character, out-write the Author of you.

8

HALFSIES

WE HAVE NOW DISCUSSED HOW THE existential approach to life has created many of our current public clashes. But very few people who read a book on Christian identity are denying Christianity at the outset. You probably believe in Jesus. You probably love Jesus. But you may still struggle with identity because it all seems to get so complicated sometimes.

I believe this is because many Christians simply don't know how much they have learned from the world. If you try to live your life just like the world is telling you to, but do it while loving Jesus and serving Him, you will most likely be living a very difficult life, or perhaps just a radically inattentive one.

The story that you write for yourself and the story that God writes for you are not dance partners. The self-created *you* and the God-created *you* do not go together like ham and eggs, peanut butter and jam, or wine and cheese. They go together more like a living body with a dead limb. Or a living head with a dead body. Or a dead body with a living hand. It is not healthy, and there is no good trajectory. And if this is what you are trying to do, it will in fact feel like wrestling and struggling and fighting and never really being at peace and in joy.

If we try to write our stories like the world does, composing our little plot points and shaping ourselves into what we think it would be neat to be, but we love Jesus, this is just making Him one more interesting plot point about us. We put our bumper sticker that says "Jesus-lover" on our little lifestyle car. Depending on how seriously we take our faith, we may have a number of more theologically rich bumper stickers, too. Like "In His service" or "Depraved Wretch." But Christ will not be managed or contained like that. If He truly bought you with His blood, He did not do so in order to get a sponsorship position in your life. He is not here to look good next to your brand. He bought your life, and you are His.

If you think that this seems like just a silly metaphor, take a minute to really reflect on the struggles that so many Christians seem to be having. We are always trying to harmonize our stories with the Christ sticker instead of submitting wholly to Him. If we are sticking bumper stickers on the backside of our life, and one of them is about Jesus but the others are "I Love Fashion," "Show Poodles Forever," or "All about essential oils," then we really ought to notice that there is something imbalanced going on. If our own little interests are the same size in our life as our Savior and our God, there are only two possibilities. One is that your Savior is becoming rather tiny—as insignificant as any other news about you. The other option is that fashion or show poodles or oils is rising to idolatrous levels in your life.

Incidentally (and a little beside the point), I believe that this is why we are such a consumer-driven culture. We are all trying to buy our identities because it is the most easily accomplished action we can think of. *Buy the stuff to be the person! Get ready for the journey you wish you were on!* A professional kitchen in the home of someone who doesn't cook is an expression of some kind of longing to be something. High performance gear for someone only thinking about dabbling is another expression of longing. And then we have people trying *not* to buy the stuff in order to shape their identities in contrast with those who do buy the stuff. The problem with the situation is not the presence or absence of the stuff itself, but rather the deep insecurity that is driving both behaviors.

This is a struggle that is reflected in many casual conversations with Christians. "I am really trying to get my focus back on God," as though you accidentally let Him get crowded out, thanks to all the other things you were interested in. You feel like it's time to rearrange the stickers on the car or on your life story board to make sure that "God, Jesus, Bible" is still visible. Or perhaps central? Are you ready to be that serious as a Christian? Maybe just a little more toward the middle? Maybe bigger than some other things? You are considering the need to rededicate your life and consider taking off some other stickers that have cropped up lately, like "Heavy Drinker" or "Gossip." (*Where did those come from anyway? I swear I never wanted that there!*)

An example of an emotional response to this kind of crisis would be these lyrics from that Carrie Underwood song which had its year in the spotlight, "Jesus Take the Wheel."

> Jesus, take the wheel
>
> Take it from my hands
>
> 'Cause I can't do this on my own
>
> I'm letting go
>
> So give me one more chance
>
> And save me from this road I'm on
>
> Jesus, take the wheel

Of course the idea of asking Jesus to carry you through something is not wrong. But the way this is all phrased assumes all manner of authority. We give Jesus permission to step in and handle our life for a moment—and that momentary grant of permission is expressed as though it is submission. As a plot point in the story we are writing about ourselves, we want to say, "And now I will allow my good friend Jesus to steer for a minute because He is better at it than I am." We think that's the extent of Christian submission—that it shows Christian humility!

This assumption is also what is behind the very common admonition to "Let go and let God." Let Him? Who exactly do you think that He is? One of the corporate sponsors at your life conference? Someone we give a little plug for at the beginning and the end of major moments? What control of your life do you actually have that you are going to turn over to the Lord for a moment? Are you really the star of the show and the main attraction? Or is He?

This kind of thinking acts like it is dealing with the big issues of submission by acknowledging that we aren't enough on our own. But it does so while trying to hang on to our own independence and authority. There is nothing comfortable about trying to be partway under the hand of God and partway in your own care and keeping. You cannot play your life as mostly yours and partly God's. Or mostly God's and partly yours. That is not what it is to be a Christian. We cannot hold onto ourselves while we try to grab onto God, too.

Christians who are struggling deeply with identity issues are getting so little help from other believers. We don't really know where to begin, so we try to help them arrange their life and identity so they can still have whatever closely held things they have found in themselves (such as being same-sex attracted) *and* Jesus, too. We have no practical understanding of what it means to have a Christian identity. We've been doing the same sticker-shuffle for years with marginally less important issues. Maybe we've found ways to keep our worldliness with us. We let Jesus drive occasionally, and our horrible entertainment standards stay in the trunk for a few minutes while He takes the wheel.

More and more is being published by other struggling Christians on this topic, but it seems to be nothing more than a bunch of ideas for arranging things in your life so you can still think you qualify as a Christian. If you want to have a rainbow pride flag and Jesus too, then it is up to you as the author of your life to try and get these things to go together. If you want to be living a promiscuous life but still assure everyone you are following Christ, you will have to do some shuffling. If you want to live a life of covetousness but still have Jesus, well, I'm sure you can find a way to fit that all in.

We Christians struggle to believe that Jesus could both love us and hate the identities we are fashioning. If He really loved us, He would be willing to be one of the presenting sponsors of whatever life we are busily creating for ourselves. He loves us, right? Aren't we whatever we make ourselves? Doesn't He love that?

I recently heard a Christian speaker address a room full of Christian women saying, "In God's eyes, you can do no wrong!" He wanted us to feel God's amazing love for us, but I am afraid what was actually expressed was our lack of love for God. When we tell each other over and over that whatever we do is precious and wonderful and glorious because God loves us, we demonstrate how little we understand ourselves and our Creator.

All of us—the gay, the straight, the same-sex attracted, the sympathetic friends, the self-righteous ones, the women looking for encouragement—all of us seem to have forgotten the very foundation of our faith.

Jesus Christ died for sinners. Jesus Christ did not come to this world and die so that you might live. That is only the partial truth, the truth that skips all the action. Jesus Christ came to this earth, struggled, suffered, and died so that you might *die*. Let that sink in. It was not His death that gave you life—His death gave you *death in*

Him. But what happened after His death? His victory over death. The resurrection. Jesus Christ died so that you might die, and He *lives* so that you might live. Your life in Christ is what happens *after* your death in Him.

There will be no resolution to these struggles in your life if you do not willingly give your self-fashioned identity to Christ that it might die. It will die anyway, so let it be in Him. And when you live, it will be in Him, too. Friends, there is no hope for you that is not Jesus. There is nothing interesting about you if it is not resurrected in Him. There is nothing *defining* about you that cannot live in Christ. Your selfishness is dead. Your lust is dead. Your need to be unique is dead. Your envy, greed, obsessions, guilts—they are all dead. Dead and gone in Christ. Stop trying to tidy them up and make them mean something, because they never will.

Total *submission* to Christ is total *life* in Christ. This is because without dying in Him you cannot live in Him. When you submit your life to Him fully, you can live in Him, fully. There is no going halfsies with death for Christians. You can't try to keep living the life that should have died in Christ. You can't arrange all your little ideas about yourself in some compatible way with your idea of Christ. Let Him have it all—what remains after that death is only life. You are no longer the author of your own identities, but rather you live in the Author and He lives in you.

9

THE WORSHIPER

IF ALL OUR FOUNDATIONAL IDEAS ARE so wrong, what are the correct answers to the questions that have been afflicting us? Who am I? What am I for? What am I really all about? Mankind is fascinated by these questions, and always has been. From the smallest child having his first philosophical thoughts, to a man or woman in the storm of a midlife crisis, to the confused regrets of the deathbed, the questions of "Who am I?" and "What am I for?" are characteristic of humanity.

In a way, it makes sense that we overwhelmingly struggle with the self because at the end of the day, everyone has one. We are eternal beings who are bound in finitude. We feel the weight of eternity without the capacity to truly understand it. We contend with a lot of unbelieving input, and we generate our own unbelieving input. We struggle with the self because the self is everywhere we go, getting its grubby little hands into everything that we do.

So while this question "Who am I?" is common, an actual answer to it is uncommon. We major on the big-philosophical-struggle side and try to minor on the reality side. This is because no one wants to hear (or give) the one-sentence summary: "Yeah. Okay. So you are a middle-aged, overweight housewife who lives in Cleveland and has trouble staying on task." Or "You are a Texas girl living in Maine who is addicted to social media. You always think you do more than you do, and have trouble with being selfish." This kind of answer is insufficient in many ways—the main reason being that *we ourselves* are insufficient.

A description of our persons isn't untrue, but it is certainly not enough to satisfy what we are looking for. If what we are at face value is enough to satisfy us, then I doubt mankind would be so obsessed with these questions. We aren't satisfied because all we see on the surface are unsatisfactory answers. This is what I mean by feeling eternity but being bound by our finitude. We know there is something bigger, and we know that somehow we are a part of it. We may be short and frequently forgetting our commitments, but somehow we know that we still *matter*.

A description of myself that even a five-year-old could give is not enough to answer this question because my heart longs for something far, far better: a deeper knowledge of myself—a deeper understanding of the whole picture of reality and how I fit in it. And surely that is greater and more glorious than the size of my pants, the actual tasks that I accomplished this last year, or my very real weaknesses. It can't really just come down to my resumé and statistics, can it?

In order to satisfy myself, who I am must in some way be greater than myself. Think about that. *My identity must be bigger than myself in order to satisfy me.* We have a yearning to know ourselves in some way that is bigger than we are. We have a need that we can't possibly fill.

There is a simple explanation for this struggle, and it is that man was created to be a worshiper. We were created with a longing and an urge that is much bigger than we are. The Westminster Confession of Faith states beautifully and simply that the chief end of man is to glorify God and enjoy Him forever. Our very purpose is to worship God. Our created purpose as humanity, as nations, as towns, as families, as individuals, is to glorify God and enjoy Him forever.

1 Corinthians 10:31 says, "Therefore, whether you eat or drink, or whatever you do, do all to the glory of God."

You are to live to the glory of God. Every minute, all of them, for His glory. Is this a sufficient answer to our hearts' questions? I believe it is. This is an answer that may leave us with more questions, but it is more questions that will in turn have real answers. This is an answer that points the way to all of the answers.

I live in Idaho, less than a mile from where I was born. I married fairly young and have seven kids. Life is busy, and I am almost always needing to cook something. I haven't traveled much, mostly because there isn't time. My work is often repetitive, but I enjoy it, and I love my people.

My hair has gotten darker with age, and I never have time to garden even though I always think I would love it. I tend to take on projects and mostly finish them, but occasionally get over-whelmed by how many things I have going that I haven't made progress on . . . Do you see how incredibly boring this is? What would I ever find here to worship? What would the point be? Let's try a more God-centered version of this.

To the glory of God, I live in Idaho, less than a mile from the place I was born. To the glory of God, I have seven children and struggle to keep up with my regular tasks. To the glory of God, I am able to laugh at my failings. To the glory of God, I want to mature and leave those faults behind. To the glory of God, my hair is darker than it used to be, and to the glory of God, it will now start to turn gray. To the glory of God, I lift up my children. To the glory of God I ask them for their forgiveness. To the glory of God, I have had phases where I had to let go of some of my "dreams," and to the glory of God, I have had phases where I needed to pick them up. To the glory of God I eat, and drink, and sleep, and love, and grow old. To the glory of God I live, and to the glory of God I will die.

In summary, it isn't really about me after all. What wonderful freedom that is! The only real value and meaning in my life is present in that wonderful phrase "To the glory of God." This is the freedom from the fear of being insufficient. I am totally insufficient, and I don't have to mind that at all. To the glory of God, I am weak. To the glory of God, I am not enough. To the glory of God, I come to Him anyway. To the glory of God, I worship and am satisfied. As David says in Psalm 3, when he is facing the consequences of his own radical sin and failures, "But You, O LORD, are a shield for me, My glory and the One who lifts up my head."

God is our glory. God is the glory of sinners, the glory of failures. God is the glory of those who submit to Him.

My need—that need that I am not big enough to fill but somehow yearn to have filled—can be filled with one thing and one thing only: His glory. When all my life is oriented around glorifying God, I see the value and glory and joy in the little. I see the Creator of all things in the details of my life. His presence there makes nothing little. Our God tells us to look to the ant because He is the one upholding the ant. So, small obedience and faithful work is glorious and honors Him. What is more, He sees it all. He commands it for His glory, and when we obey, He (the Infinite, Almighty Maker of heaven and earth) takes pleasure in us.

My need to know "me" gets swallowed up in the glory of the One who made me—the One who holds me in His hand. If you would know yourself, seek your God. Know your God, and you will know yourself. Live to His glory and you will be living fully to your own potential. Live for His glory and He will lift up your head.

10

PLANTING FLAGS

ONE OF THE MOST GLORIOUS THINGS about seeing ourselves as worshipers is that it puts all the events of our own lives in perspective. This happens in two ways.

First, it gives us a realistic sense of how *little* all our troubles are. We are the worshipers, and we are not the worshiped. We are characters, and He is the Author. God is great, and we are not. It puts our little concerns next to all the great things of life, and we can see them more clearly in the light of what really matters.

However, second, it gives us a realistic sense of how *big* our lives are, because it ties our little details into the great, good story. We are only worshipers, but we are worshipers of the Living God. We have our hands full of little troubles, but they are little troubles that *matter* to the Maker of the universe. With this perspective, we can both see that this is a small offering and also that it is a great God we serve. His care over our lives makes our lives reflect His greatness. In other words, knowing yourself to be a worshiper both keeps you humble and makes you glorious.

To a worshiper of God there is always this kind of comfort from 2 Corinthians: "For our light affliction, which is but for a moment, is working for us a far more exceeding and eternal weight of glory" (4:17).

Whatever troubles us in our lives is only a fragment compared to the weight of the glory—and that glory will not be momentary, but rather eternal. Everything is little here, everything is momentary—but it means great glory later. It is small and glorious at the same time. Passing and petty, eternal and profound.

There is one great story in the whole history of the world. A story that starts with the darkness on the face of the deep, and proceeds through thousands of years as the story of our God and His chosen people. It is a story of courage and faithfulness, idolatry and destruction, amazing glory and unspeakable shame.

The most important thing about this story, a thing which many Christians today have forgotten, is that the story is not finished. This is our story. This is the beginning of you and who you are and who you will be eternally. Your story begins with the words, "In the beginning, God." And while the canon of Scripture is closed, the story of God and His people is most certainly not. Your life today is part of this great and glorious story. Your trouble at work, your need to clean the bathroom and make dinner, your difficult conversation with a friend—this is all part of the greatest story. How you handle losing your basketball game or finding out you are pregnant is all part of the great story God is writing.

Does that seem a little overly precious to you? It isn't. It is overtly biblical. Consider these words from Scripture and what they say about us: "You also, as living stones, are being built up a spiritual house, a holy priesthood, to offer up spiritual sacrifices acceptable to God through Jesus Christ" (1 Pet. 2:5).

We are the living temple because we are connected to and held together by the Living Cornerstone, Jesus Christ. God is building this temple in His Son, and you are part of that.

When people who do not know Christ seek to craft their own stories to make themselves something of value, they will always run into this impossible crisis: you are little. Your life is short. What if you get cut down in your prime by something you never wanted, like cancer? You will be cut down, eventually, by something. Life is difficult, and things happen that are well out of your control. If your whole value is tied up in your story *only*, then your whole value can be taken away in an instant by a single disaster or difficult times.

When Christians who know their value in Christ and their place in this one great narrative face such things, they can still see the glory in it. The humbling in your little story connects directly to the humbling of Christ for your salvation. Your small victories declare His great ones—your victory over fussiness at your children *connects* to His victory over death. Your death, when it comes, will only be the beginning of eternal life. Your death could come in your prime, or *before* your prime, and you would be no less *you* in Christ. Your story would be no smaller, your value unaffected. You could die in infancy and be *no less important*. You will still live eternally in Christ and need have no fear of the grave.

I've said that as Christians we may not craft our story as the world does—climbing the hierarchy of needs, using others as stepping-stones to become our best, most fulfilled selves. But Christians can and in fact *should* seek to work on their own story, but we should do so in the way that God tells us to. That way is called obedience. We make ourselves stepping-stones for God's purposes. We lay ourselves low, in submission to Him, and in that way He shapes us into something greater. We do this through acts of faithfulness, and spiritual sacrifices that are acceptable to God (1 Pet. 2:5). How exactly is that done?

One way that is done is through what I would call planting flags. It is moments of overt recognition that what you are doing, you are doing for the glory of God. Think of Joshua and his glorious words, "As for me and my house, we will serve the LORD" (Josh. 24:15). That was a flag planted. That was faithfulness and intention declared. A spiritual offering to God.

A normal Christian has many opportunities for similar declarations in all sizes of territories. Maybe you are struggling with getting your finances in order. Offer it to God. Plant a flag. "Lord, we intend to glorify You in the way we spend our money. Equip us to do so more and more." Or maybe you have a difficult morning with small children ahead of you. "Lord, accept my work here as part of Your great work in the kingdom. Make this small offering matter by making it great in Your hands. Glorify my work that Your name may be praised." Maybe the territory you really need to plant a flag on is your past. Maybe grievous sins hang over you, and what you need most is to look at them and say, "All this belongs to my King Jesus and is forgiven for His glory and my good. May He use it in His kingdom, may His name be praised, and may I grow ever more like Him."

Recently I had a major hospitality moment coming on me faster than seemed reasonable. You know that terrible combination of feeling exhausted *and* frantic? That was me—very urgent, but at the same time much too tired to effectively get all the laundry off the dining room table and the floors clean. Very predictably, this kind of moment leads to frustrations and pettiness and an overall lack of lighthearted joy. As the clock was winding down, my heart was not at all at peace. It took me far too long to plant a flag, but finally I said out loud, "Lord, be my guest." There it was! Submission, joy, relief. *That* was what I was doing right then. Not fussing or being tested on housekeeping or serving food for critics. I was showing hospitality to the Lord and for the Lord.

Planting flags has a wonderful ability to clear the air and get yourself back on track. *I am here for You, Lord; use me.* While this is certainly simple and something that many Christians already do instinctively, it is important to think on it and intentionally practice planting flags that claim your life for Jesus. It is fundamental to how we see our lives, what we think we are here for, and how we will go on living. The constant declaration that our life is His and we are here as worshipers is a way of referencing the true Story throughout our smaller stories. We are part of it. We know we are, and we can act in the confidence of people who know themselves truly.

11

A NEW GLORY

WHEN WE TALK ABOUT THIS KIND OF
obedience and the glory that comes about when
regular Christians obey Christ in a regular way,
doing regular things, in regular time, with regular skills and abilities, this thought often comes
to mind: This may all be fine, but surely there
must be more. So I told the Lord that I wanted
to honor Him today at breakfast with my fussy
children, but can this morning really be meaningful? I committed this day to God's glory, but
still it is just this day, and it is boring and rainy

and drab. This cannot be all. God might want regular obedience, but He must certainly want *exceptional* obedience, too. If He is a great God, He must want great people honoring Him with great faith, great works, and great ideas. But here I am so very boring and normal and quiet. What about accomplishing great things *for real*? What about declaring the glory of God in a bigger way than regular, normal obedience? Surely God wants that too, right? He can't really be content with a bunch of Christians just doing the normal all the time.

This little mind-game of ours reveals a major misleading assumption: we think great obedience and exceptional performances are generally driven by discontent with the normal and the everyday. We think any person who accomplishes exceptional things for the kingdom must have graduated beyond the regular obedience in regular life to be allowed to enter the more hallowed ground of obedience that matters. Surely they don't have time for the normal anymore, because God is using them in bigger ways, and we long to go ahead like them and not have to worry about the regular obedience anymore. Forget fiddling around trying to deal with this lame attitude I am having today; there are bigger forces of darkness to quell! I'm going to change the world, not wrestle with my own sin nature!

Because of this mistaken assumption, we let go of the very means we have for doing something that can (and can't help but) make a bigger impact. People who do something monumental for the kingdom usually do it because it was simply the next step in the path they had been walking along faithfully for some time. He who is faithful with a little will be faithful with much. When you embrace the work that God has put in front of you today in order to do your duty and glorify Him, He will always give you more seeds to plant. You must say in your everyday living, "This is more than enough for me, thank You, Lord!" When we plant the seeds of our obedience in Christ, the harvest will not fail.

In 1 Corinthians 15:58, Paul writes, "Therefore, my beloved brethren, be steadfast, immovable, always abounding in the work of the Lord, knowing that your labor is not in vain in the Lord."

Isn't that just lovely? Your labor in the Lord is not in vain. Things are happening with your labors so long as they are in the Lord. No obedience to the Lord will ever go out into the void to continue to be useless into eternity. Things are

happening; nothing is in vain. Your small obedience means something.

This is encouragement to do something. And
what is that something? *Be steadfast; be immovable. Stand firm. Let nothing move you!* Let
no feelings of unimportance or insignificance
sway you from the course of this very simple
obedience. Be in the Lord. Labor in the Lord.
Let all the importance and value of your work
be done by the Lord, in His time, and according
to His purposes.

Whenever I see a verse that begins with
therefore, I think of what my grandfather always
asked in Bible studies. "What is the *therefore*
there for?" When someone makes a statement
that begins with *therefore*, we can know that
whatever preceded it is the reason for it. If you
said you were hot, therefore you were going to
open the window, it is safe to say that you are
opening the window because you are hot.

1 Corinthians 15:58 says you know your labor
is not in vain. Why do we know this? Let's walk
through it. *Because* of all the things that came
before. But what came before? A big discussion
of the resurrection. If we believe in the resurrection, then we can be steadfast and immovable, having confidence that all our labor is not

in vain. We believe in the resurrection, so we can do these things (remain steadfast, laboring in the Lord).

We believe that Jesus Christ rose from the dead, *therefore*. Therefore we can have fruitful and faithful lives. Therefore, we cannot be moved by little distractions like our own emotions. We are anchored to something infinitely more important, permanent, and true.

So this hunger for only important obedience or important faithfulness reveals that we are not actively believing in the resurrection. But we are told to see all of these kinds of small obediences through the lens of the most shocking event of human history—the Resurrection. The obedience of contentment and gratitude will not stay small. It will not continue on, just you and your tiny obedience, forever. In the hands of God, it will go through the grave. It will change from you and your little offerings to you and your wild fruit. The Christian embraces every small opportunity to small obedience. Why is that? Because we serve the God who makes the small things great. Our small things, given to Him, will be great. You can trust Him for that.

We tend to think of the virtue of contentment as a great dud, as though it is the virtue that does not want anything and has no opinions. Contentment, meaning not too hot, not too cold, not thirsty, not hungry. Basically, the most boring emotion that can be had. We think thankfulness is similarly passive. But contentment and gratitude, some of the smallest seeds, grow some of the biggest trees. These are some of the wildest forces for change in this world. Contentment says to God, "Where You put me, I will honor You. Where You send me, I will go. Where You are, I will be glad." Gratitude says to God that you accept what He has given you to do, and you will do it, not grudgingly, but with joy.

Do you see that? "Wherever You take me, Lord, my cup will be full." How can a Christian be truly content and thankful and joyful in situations that appear by all accounts to be mundane and boring? Because the Christian's cup is not full of difficult situations or important opportunities or even feelings. The Christian's cup is full of Christ. Always full, always overflowing.

How would that kind of contentment be useful? It is not only useful, it is incredibly powerful. Because nothing preaches Jesus more than people who say with their lives, "I have Him, so I need nothing more." When your happiness and your hope and your purpose are not hanging on anything but Christ, then you are completely free to enjoy whatever situation you find yourself in. A Christian who is living in the joy of the Lord can truly know that his situation is not beneath the notice of Christ. How can they know? Because He is Himself there with them. He Himself is taking their obedience through death into resurrection.

This longing to do something *important* that would *matter* is just another form of unbelief. Every Christian is always in the middle of the spiritual action, whether being faithful as a mother at home nursing babies, as a single person pursuing their studies, as a missionary, as a worker at the local laundromat, as a CEO, or as a janitor. *You are always in the midst of your own most important spiritual work.* Your hands are always full of God's seeds, if you will just plant them.

Many years ago, I went to a conference across the country because my dad had been invited to speak there. I was a senior in high school and I didn't know anyone. Most of the kids were from the region and came in youth groups, or at least in clusters of people who all knew each other. Now, one thing you should know about me is that on any spectrum in the world I would be considered outgoing. But this was still a socially tiring kind of situation, and I did not feel like working at it. I remember standing in the registration line for those of us with the last name that started with W and looking around, being bored, feeling like this was a bad idea, and really not wanting to bother with anything. In the kindness of God, I do remember being convicted that I probably ought to overcome my poor mood and be friendly. And so, in a quiet, very little and unimportant way, I obeyed. I know that the Lord uses our obedience all the time for His purposes, but in this one incident I can see the trail—the actual impact—that this one pitiful piece of obedience had. I interrupted the girls in front of me and introduced myself. We hit it off right away, and within the hour I was trying to talk these sisters into moving across the country to come to New Saint Andrews College with me. What I didn't know, what I could not have in any way anticipated, was how that one small piece of obedience, which was not hard or important, would change a lot of lives.

God used that moment to change the trajectory of a whole family. Those girls, the oldest of seven siblings, became the first to move to Idaho. And their siblings followed. To meet spouses. To raise children. Twenty-something children are growing up in our community here, now, because those girls I interrupted became dear friends. Because our last names started with W, and because the Lord convicted me of a little stupid selfishness. What is really remarkable is it was also an answer to their mother's prayers. She had not been able to convince them to consider moving to Idaho for college, and the Lord answered her prayers by putting me there, bored out of my mind and not in the mood at all.

These things happen all the time, but we seldom see it all. I don't know why I remember it so clearly, but I have always been thankful that the Lord saw fit to show me how the simplest acts of little faithfulness are never wasted in His hands. Who was my attitude affecting at that moment? Not a solitary person other than myself. But who was affected by my obedience? Hundreds so far! Thousands? Probably. In the future it will easily be ten thousands.

But what would have happened if I had gone to that conference with a stated goal of changing thousands of lives? I will roll in there and shake up everything! I will influence people and change the course of their lives! It will be amazing! Watch this!

Nope, it wasn't my goal that accomplished anything. It wasn't my instincts or perfect timing. It wasn't my insight, my ideas, or my execution of a friendly introduction. It was just simple obedience in the hands of the Lord. Normal kindness overcoming normal selfishness. God can accomplish great things with the very little things that we offer in obedience.

We don't have to set out to change the world. We set out to obey the Lord, and even the simplest actions can leave glorious marks of obedience forever.

12

HANGING ON

CHRISTIANS KNOW THAT WE ARE called to a higher purpose. We know that our lives matter. We know that God has something that is just right for us to be doing. Or at least we *should* believe this because it is perfectly right and true, founded on the very clear teaching of Scripture. So why are so many Christians still looking for their purpose? Why are we mostly not clear on who we are, or what God is doing in our lives? If it is true that God has this perfect purpose for us, why would we be staggering around looking for it in this most imperfect kind of a way?

If God's plan is perfect, is trying really hard to figure out where we fit in really a part of it? We behave as though God is the most efficient travel agent and the whole trip is planned from beginning to end and everything is on sticky-notes for you in the most thoughtful way. The food is exactly what you might want and need at every point, and every moment not only has been scheduled but has been planned to be ultimately good for you! It will all work together for glory and for good! What more could we ever ask for?

The one hitch is that it seems to be totally up to you to guess when it starts and what the transportation will be. You believe in faith that God has planned this meaningful and perfect and fulfilling path for you to follow, but for some reason He has not taken the final step of telling you where to start or what to pack.

Because we believe this kind of thing, you will find many Christians wandering aimlessly in the train stations and airports of this life, waiting for the magic clue to drop from Heaven and get them started on the magical journey to their spiritual calling that they trust is out there. Good on them for trusting that it's there, but surely this isn't the way that purposeful lives and focused callings should be starting out.

This same confusion leads people to look for their own path to honoring God with their lives. They can be fooled into thinking that even their own sin might be the path that will lead them there. Maybe the sin is the clue they need to find their strengths and understand their purpose. They neglect the obedience *now* for the obedience that will surely be more glorious in the future.

Is this accurate? Is this the way that our lives are supposed to go? Does it glorify God to have His people wandering so aimlessly through life, even if they believe that what is happening to them is happening for a greater purpose? Are all the Christian moms choosing to stay at home just until they get their ticket to something that might really matter? Are we working in meaningless jobs wondering when God will appear to us and show us what we were really made for?

Some want to help you find this calling. They believe that this trip will be everything you ever wanted in your life and all the purpose you obviously need, so they set themselves up as mini travel agents. They will help you decipher your personality and your gifts, and they will attempt to book you a journey that starts where you are currently standing and takes you to the beginning of a life with more purpose. Their general idea is that all your history and your trials and your natural inclinations are clues to what God has been making you for.

When we do this, we are trying to cobble together a list of clues that will get us to the start of what God intended for us. But man! What a lot of pressure for all of us. And what a lot of despair. What a lot of doubt. What if you accidentally got onto the trip that was intended for someone else? And there is often good reason to believe you may have! Because it isn't all fun and games. The food doesn't seem to be exactly to your taste. The trip is not at all what you would have planned for yourself. You do not feel like your best self in this life you are in. Turns out we are not impressed with this whole concept.

These things combine to confuse us in really monumental ways. We can start wondering if we are actually believers. Because surely, if we were, this would all be making better sense. Or we can start doubting that God does actually work all things out according to His purposes and for our good. How could His purposes and our good include cancer? Or car accidents? Or so many things that are so obviously against our taste, our desires, our gifts? How could years of what feels like pointlessness be part of a perfect plan? We feel like we got tricked onto this life path when we weren't cynical enough to avoid it, and we wonder what kind of God would have done this to us?

When we do this, we justify our discontent by telling ourselves that God made us for more. What we need is to shake off the things around us that annoy us so much, shake off our trials and our burdens, and step higher into our better purposes. If we still believe God and trust Him, we assume that we made a wrong turn and that we shouldn't be here after all. To honor Him more, we need to find our *new* start of our *new* journey, one that will really take advantage of our special skills and desires and gifts, all the things that we perceive make us really uniquely ourselves.

None of these is the biblical approach. Here's the good news: the way we can know that we are doing what we are supposed to be doing is actually very simple. Are you obeying God? Are you honoring Him? Are you being content and rejoicing in your lot? Congratulations! You have tremendous purpose and clarity and calling.

This is it.

Now, I want to be clear on something. When we have tremendous insight into the workings of God in our lives, when we can see clearly how He used us or our circumstances or our gifts, or even when we see the same things in the lives of other Christians, we are seeing in retrospect. In retrospect, we see how being faithful in that little moment led to great things. In retrospect, we see how God worked in a moment that did not feel important or critical or planned. When we look back, we see Him in it.

But here is the problem. We don't see what is really happening at the time. We don't feel like great things are happening even when they are. I imagine there were martyrs who felt at the last that if only they had been doing a better job as a Christian, they would not have wasted their life like this. Think of that! People whose stories we still tell, whose faith we are still encouraged by, probably wondered if it mattered at all at the time.

Doing incredibly glorious things does not always feel glorious. In fact, I think it seldom does. The widow with her two mites probably did not feel glorious as she offered her little all. Christ glorified her faithfulness with His acceptance of her offering. When the woman came and anointed Jesus with an alabaster jar full of oil, she was shamed by the disciples. Jesus told them that not only was this embarrassing moment of hers actually lovely, but that wherever the Gospel went, so would the story of what she did. It would be told in memory of her. And it is. We can still offer our everything to Christ, however small it seems, and have Him glorify it forever. It is what He does.

Years ago, when my parents purchased some land, Dad bought a field and brush mower. It was huge and self-powered. It could mow over saplings three inches thick. It was a beast. And when you mowed with it, you felt yourself jogging along behind a thing that was well out of control as you did your noble best not to mow down the orchard. I have thought of this many times as an example of what faithfulness feels like. It feels like out of control. It feels like thanking God breathlessly for things that you think were a bad idea. It feels like struggling to keep up and being sure that you aren't doing a great job. It feels like not really seeing the vision for what you are doing. And yet, whenever you look over your shoulder, where you expect to see the devastation of your poorly executed job, what you see instead is a beautiful garden growing. *Faithfulness does not feel like what it is accomplishing.*

We have gotten so consumed with feelings needing to be pleasant that we have discarded the generally unpleasant feelings of faithfulness. It doesn't *feel* good, so it cannot *be* good. But discarding the feelings of faithfulness discards the fruits of it. And the fruit is all the glory and purpose and calling you could ever need or want. It only seems unpleasant for a moment, until we learn how to see in faith.

Far from living a life of waiting and expectation, wondering when our journey of a lifetime is going to start, the Christian life should be one of almost breathless and constant obedience. What honors God in this conversation? How do I share the Gospel with my co-worker who desperately needs it? What should I do when a friend turns on me? How do I discipline my toddler in a way that honors God? How do I submit to my husband on principle and not emotion? How do I love my wife like Christ instead of selfishly? What should I do about this hospitality opportunity that I don't want to take? How do

I lay my life down for my friends here? What does God think of this movie I am watching?

When we embrace the fact that *obedience now* is always the calling of a Christian, we find that we have more than enough to do. We are not to be the lost travelers hanging out at all the bus stations in life looking for our potential ticket to something that matters. Read the Word. Obey the Word. Obey it *now*. Obey it *again*.

This is a call to grab the handle of the great gardening machine called obedience and let the glory of God power you through a great number of three–inch tree trunks. Hang on, obey Him, watch the chips fly, feel them sting on your shins, and occasionally look behind you to see the beauty that God is accomplishing in your obedience, because it will be genuinely glorious.

Laugh at your own small part in His glorious design. Rejoice in your Savior who does much with your little, and simply hang on to Him with a willing spirit.

13

GLORY GIVERS

"NOT UNTO US, O LORD, NOT UNTO US, but to Your name give glory, because of Your mercy, because of Your truth." This is the glorious first verse of Psalm 115. Christians are wonderfully free from the need to self-worship. Do we want glory? Of course, but not for us! We are not seeking the glory for ourselves but for our God. To Him be the glory, because He is worthy. We glorify Him for His love and faithfulness. This should be our orientation as we are rightly driven to pursue glory. We have a natural, God-given desire for glory, but it must have a healthy purpose. Glory to give, not glory to hoard. Glory to pass on.

This brings tremendous freedom. We do not struggle to be glorious, but we struggle to give glory. Being glorious is for God. Giving glory is a human task. This is what we are created for anyway. Being glorious is out of our reach, because it is the wrong goal.

Think of two things that work together—let's say the pipes that carry water and a sink. The pipes can do an amazing job of moving water. But they cannot hold it like the sink. Much like that, humans are made to be traffickers in glory. We bring glory, we give glory, we reflect glory. But we are terrible receivers of it. We cannot hold glory because it was never meant for us. We are given glory to give it to our Maker. This is our task. This is our purpose. If a pipe has no outlet for the water, it is pointless and it will burst. When a person receives glory and has no place to give it, they will burst. When they have only a little glory that they don't know what to do with, they go sadly stagnant. Nothing to see here, no real stories, no real trajectory or hope or purpose, just a little bit of dead water. Or, one big burst of water and then flooding. I only have a little, and I am doing nothing with it. Or, I have much, but it has destroyed me. These are not good options.

Worship is the way we give glory. Men and women who are not driven about by the world's definitions of glory worship their God in the beauty of holiness. These are men and women who are at peace with each other's success and who are free of the bizarre burden of self-love. Consequently, they are much lovelier, and are able to gracefully accept their own insufficiencies with joy and laughter.

If you know that your purpose is to glorify God, and God Himself gave you some physical failing, then you can know that this failing is not keeping you from doing what God wants you to do. You are free from worrying that you aren't enough. You aren't! None of us is! And that is good news. We weren't made to be gods, we were made to be worshipers—a job we are well suited to.

Being oriented to glorifying God is the simplest way to discern His will in your life. You want to glorify Him, so you glorify Him in your obedience. You do what He said. You obey His Word—this is love. And when a decision or a question comes up in your life—you lay it out before Him. You seek His pleasure. You ask Him to be glorified in your behavior and consequently your behavior is shaped by your goal. When you are oriented to glorifying God, hard decisions are made simple. What is obedient here? Who should I trust? What can I do that will glorify God through my obedience now? We don't need to measure the costs and bet against the odds. We need to glorify and obey.

The way the Bible speaks of glory is not the way that we would. Do you think that you can eat or drink gloriously? And yet Scripture tells us to do exactly that, and whatever else you do in your whole life, to the glory of God (1 Cor. 10:31). Breathe to the glory of God. Sit in silence to the glory of God. Tie your shoes to the glory of God. Take a nap to the glory of God. Enjoy your friend's success to the glory of God.

Now chances are pretty good that most of these things seem somewhat silly to you. How exactly, you are thinking, is this routine part of my life glorifying God?

This reveals something about the way in which we stumble away from our most fundamental truths and realities. You are a living, breathing, thinking, moving creation. God is sustaining you in your every moment. Your heart does not beat without His direction. Your lungs cannot breathe outside of His will. The fact that you are present in this world at all is a testimony to His awesome power—so how could the smallest things in your life not be part of bringing glory to God? You yourself are only here because of His glory. So your every behavior should also be oriented around that fundamental creational relationship.

Does all of this trafficking in glory but keeping none for ourselves sound sort of sad? Does it sound like we are getting the raw end of the deal? Why does God want the glory from even our smallest actions, like taking a sip of water? Doesn't He want us to be happy and fulfilled?

Once again we see how we are fundamentally confused about ourselves. We think that God is taking something away from us that we would like to have. But the reality is that we get sick on glory. If we try to keep it, it kills us. But what God gives to us in exchange, we thrive on: "You will show me the path of life; in Your presence is fullness of joy; at Your right hand are pleasures forevermore" (Ps. 16:11).

This psalm shows us what we receive when we are near to God. We receive direction—we know the way because we are on the path of life. And on that path we receive fullness of joy and pleasures forevermore.

Is there any human on the planet who would say that we do not thrive on clarity of purpose, joy, and pleasure? Those are ours when we are near to God.

How could we be nearer to God than to be constantly glorifying Him? Learning to live your life as a sacrifice is learning to be as close to God as you possibly can be, all of the time. This is the point. Be near to Him when you eat your dinner for His glory. Be near to Him when you take your dog on a walk. Be near to Him when you do anything you do, all the days of your life.

This arrangement for us to be glory-givers is not a one-way street of giving where we do the bulk of the work and God benefits off of us. The pitiful little offerings we make to glorify God are answered back to us in an abundant river of mercy and joy and pleasure. God did not create us to receive things from us; rather, He created to give. He gives Himself. He gives mercy. He gives joy. He gives purpose. He gives pleasure. And He gives us much when we glorify Him.

The command to be constantly glorifying our God is essentially a command to be living in constant joy, with constant clarity of purpose

and constant pleasures forevermore. Only to a
sick heart could this arrangement sound like
bondage. God tells us to give Him the things
that we shouldn't have, things that will destroy
us if we keep them, and then we receive from
His hand the things we need–things that give
us life and hope and joy. Give away the glory,
but keep the joy. Give away the glory, but keep
the purpose and the pleasure.

We are made to traffic in glory that we might
live in joy.

14

ASKING FOR LESS

PSALM 115 MOVES FROM THE GLORY OF God to the subject of worshiping idols. They have eyes, it says, but cannot see. They have mouths, but cannot speak. They are not the powerful gods that the maker of them hopes they will be. There is nothing there but emptiness. "Those who make them will be like them, and so will all who trust in them" (v. 8, NIV).

This is a shattering blow to idolatry. It is repeated in various ways throughout Scripture. Hosea 9:10 says it this way: "They became an abomination like the thing they loved." Those who make the gods of emptiness will themselves be empty. Trusting in a god that is nothing more than an illusion will only make you feel like and become an illusion. Do you feel like you have eyes but cannot see, ears but cannot hear, a mouth but cannot taste? Haven't you heard people describe their own depression or anxiety or purposelessness in this way? It is a recurring theme of almost everyone's nightmare: the inability to be heard, run, or see.

The only answer is that you must turn to the Living God. You are already on your knees, but it might not be in front of the right altar. Your god is not sufficient. Reorient yourself to worshiping the Almighty God, and you will be transformed.

When we faithfully worship the Living God, what do we become like? We become more like Him. As we imitate Christ, we become more Christlike. This is the goal of sanctification and the Christian walk. But there is more to it than that.

Remember that man is made in the image of God. God made man out of dirt and His own breath. We are His. And when we worship Him rightly, we become more and more like Him. We become more and more like the image we were made to reflect. So it is in our worship of God that we are made ever more like Him, and consequently ever more like our true selves. This was the intended plan.

Because we are made in the image of God, it is not difficult to see that increasing in our knowledge of Him is increasing in our understanding of our selves. How do we become more and more like Him? Through worship we obey Him, and through our obedience, we worship Him. It follows that those same things, obedience and worship, make us more and more like ourselves. Obey God to be yourself. Worship God to find yourself. This is the plain teaching of Scripture, which is what makes it so strange that many Christians have never been taught this basic truth.

As a culture we love the idea of a superfood. Tell us about the food that does so much more than all the other foods! We want that kind of high-octane fuel that will power us up to much more energetic living. Think of obedience the same way—it is the superfood of the believer. When you read a biography of a famous Christian, it's hard to even imagine how they had so much commitment, so much willpower, so much joy.

The reality is that they were living in and on obedience. They were living on a spiritual superfood which gave them spiritual super strength. The nature of obedience is not what we think it is. We have been thinking of it as some kind of difficult pellet of humility that we occasionally have to eat when things get really rough. But the truth is that obedience is far more like a perfect fruit that meets all of our needs. It quenches our thirst and provides us with sustained energy. It brings us closer to our God and provides clear direction and joy for us. If all this is true, why do we consistently avoid eating it? For the worst possible reason: because it is more than we wanted.

This passage in 1 Corinthians states the problem perfectly: "For Jews request a sign, and Greeks seek after wisdom; but we preach Christ crucified, to the Jews a stumbling block and to the Greeks foolishness, but to those who are called, both Jews and Greeks, Christ the power of God and the wisdom of God" (1:22–24).

Think about this passage with me. The Jews were requesting a sign, the Greeks were seeking wisdom. Jesus did not answer any of their searching. Why? Because they were looking for less than He was. They searched for a sign, but

Jesus was not a sign! He was the actual power of God. The unbelieving Jews continued searching for *clues* that there might be power somewhere and rejected the *actual* power of God right in front of them. Jesus crucified was to them a stumbling block, because they were looking all around Him for clues.

And what about the Greeks? They wanted less than Jesus, too. They were seeking after wisdom in such a way that they rejected the actual, incarnate Wisdom as foolishness. The Greeks liked the idea of a perfect wisdom that was pure and out of our reach in the world of the forms. They could not imagine perfect wisdom in the flesh, so they dismissed it as foolishness. They wanted something less real, something easier to control, something less accessible than a crucified Lord.

So it often is with us. We would rather continue our quest for our identity, looking for clues all around us, for those little indicators of who we might be and what we might be here for, rather than placing all our hope in the ultimate identity that we have. Christ crucified is more than everything we ask for. He is beyond enough. He is the actual power of God and wisdom of God. He is all in all. And yet we so often say, "That isn't quite what I am looking for. Give me something a little . . . less."

You may be thinking that you have never said that. Because, laid out there bare like that, very few Christians dare to say that Jesus is "not enough" for them. So let's look at some of the very mundane, more familiar ways that we do this. What are some of the most common wants we have as we struggle through our lives?

We might say we are just really, really needing a break. We need a chance to recuperate and relax. A little rest? We are stressed and want some time off. What is Jesus in this situation? He, the incarnate Son of God, is our everlasting rest. An everlasting rest and peace has already been given to us in Christ, and we are still looking for short-term, unsatisfying rest. Why? Because we are asking for less. We are turning aside from this monumental gift to say that it isn't quite the thing we meant. Worse, we might be thinking of Jesus as another item on our to-do list. Another thing that makes us feel weary.

This is the reality: Christ is more than you ever wanted. He answers the need you are feeling around in the dark to fill, and He answers it in a way that will deal with it forever. In fact, He answers whatever need you have in such a way that you are transformed forever.

What if we are looking for a little appreciation and recognition? We might be trying to find ways in which our work matters. We might be resenting the backstage role we have at the office, the less-than-famous artist that we have become. We might be at home with our children, wishing any grownups cared about what we are sacrificing. Or we might be unmarried and wishing we had anyone at all who wanted to know what we were doing all day. We look for something little to cheer us up. Maybe, if someone brought us a coffee and said they knew how hard we were working and that it mattered, we would feel better. We think we would be satisfied if there was just a sign that anyone cared, or if anyone was thoughtful enough to notice that we are tired because we have been working so hard. We want someone to tell us how this is such important and hard work we are doing. Maybe we would feel better if anyone knew and appreciated what a long day we had. We are looking to be known and to be loved. But is this a need that Jesus does not fill?

We want a little indicator that our lives matter to someone. Is the death, burial, and resurrection of Jesus Christ the Son of God not enough for us? Does that not show us that we are valued and loved in an authoritative way? Has He not told us that He knows every hair on our heads? He knows us and understands us to such an extent that absolutely nothing in our lives is outside His knowledge. Once again, this is more than what we were looking for. We are urged to cast *all* our cares on Him, for He cares for us. And yet we look around and wonder why there is no one willing to help us bear our burdens. We wanted a thoughtfully timed coffee, not cleansing blood and the everlasting arms. We wanted someone to say, "I care about you" on a post-it note, not someone to give their life for us. Do you see how we are in possession of more than what we are looking for? We are wasting our time looking around for support and encouragement when we have Christ. We want to drink hesitantly from a sippy cup of comfort while God offers us the opportunity to stand under a Niagara Falls of glory.

We have eternal forgiveness, and we seek cheap validation. We have an omnipotent, omnipresent, and eternal God, and we just wish someone knew what we were going through. We want to matter, but we are part of the very body of Christ. When we begin to worship our ideas of support and love and encouragement and start orienting ourselves around those, we become shallow and short-term people. But when we look to Christ, our shallow problems are completely overshadowed by the size of our answers. Christ is all in all. In Him there is no room for neediness.

It is as though we are children at the dinner table, and God has put a table loaded with food in front of us. But instead of eating it, we are pining away–praying even! *"I am so hungry, Lord. Please just give me some little thing. A crust of bread would be enough. I am starving, Lord. Send someone to feed me!"* What kind of nonsense is this? We already have more than the things we are asking for. We have the Bread of Life. We have all the answers already because we have Christ. We have Him crucified, and we have Him at the right hand of God the Father, reigning. What more could we possibly be asking for?

Think of some longing that you have, something that sounds perfectly normal to long for or to wish for. Now look at it honestly. Do you seek after riches? You, who are a child of the King? Do you look for hope? You, who have been saved from death to life? Do you long to be attractive? You, who have been chosen individually by God to live in Him and for Him? Do you want recognition? You, whose hairs are numbered by the Living God? Do you want purpose? You, whose God has promised that every single thing in your life will work together for your good? You, whose Father has sent you out to accomplish His heavenly work here on earth?

The Jews looked for a sign of power and rejected the actual power of God. The Greeks sought for wisdom and rejected the incarnate wisdom of God as foolishness. And we, in the same way, seek after identity when what we have been given in Christ is the sort of identity, purpose, clarity, and calling that swallows up every other need.

The greatest thing that we can do to better understand ourselves is to lay all our restlessness at His feet. We need to open our hands that are full of little requests and little needs, and drop them all so that we might, with both hands and whole hearts, embrace the One who is so much more. Look to Christ. He is not just enough; He is more. He is everlasting joy, everlasting forgiveness, everlasting love. In this life we will never be able to fully grasp what He is offering us. But we can begin. We can lay hold of Him. We can let go of our cheap substitutes and our petty needs and embrace Christ crucified. To some it may be a stumbling block or foolishness. But to those who are in Him, it is the very power of God, and the very wisdom of God, and the very essence of your life.

LOST BOYS

I FREQUENTLY TELL MY KIDS THAT ALL you really need to know for your whole life is contained in this rich passage in Psalm 100: "Know that the Lord, He is God; it is He who has made us, and not we ourselves; we are His people and the sheep of His pasture" (v. 3).

The world's approach to finding answers about questions of the self is entirely at odds with the Christian doctrine of creation *ex nihilo* (out of nothing). The divide begins right there at that creational line. The Christian belief is that God made you out of nothing, without help from anything or anyone else, and He did so intentionally. The world's belief is that you are basically a wild accident and must make yourself if you want to be anything. The Christian belief is that your life, all of it, is meaning-full. The world's belief is that it is all ultimately meaning-less. The Christian belief is that you cannot make yourself. The world's belief is that only you can make or decide things about your true self. The Christian belief is that we belong here as intentional creations who have a relationship to our Creator. The world's belief is that we only answer to ourselves. At every turn, the world has a wrong answer.

We are constantly hearing the teaching of the world. They write their messages into every show, they preach their false gospel of false hope in every movie, magazine article, book, Instagram account, and decorative letterboard. It is hard to do so much as buy a pair of tweezers without being witnessed to about the power of your own beauty and the importance of believing in yourself.

It is the ongoing nature of the world's quest for meaning and purpose that has muddled many a Christian. How many athletes, politicians, and entrepreneurs have taken entire interviews to tell us that we just have to believe in ourselves? We hear this said often enough that we start to think it must be true, especially when such successful people say it. If you run into thirty people in one day who mention that they like your purple pants, you might start to think you are wrong in thinking your pants are black. The world repeats their misguided beliefs so often that we all start to assume that there really must be something to them. This is the logical fallacy of repetition, and it is the idea behind brainwashing. We start to believe what we hear often, even when it is really dumb or clearly untrue.

There is a shard of truth in the exhortations to believe you can do things and thus not quit when you could have worked a little harder and succeeded (e.g., Col. 3:23 or Prov. 13:4). But "believing in yourself" is an entirely different proposition: it's a core belief of a false gospel. Self-belief might sound innocuous enough in athlete interviews at the Olympics, but remember that the core belief of our faith is to believe on the Lord Jesus Christ. Romans 10:9–10 is a perfect summary: "That if you confess with your mouth the Lord Jesus and believe in your heart that

God has raised Him from the dead, you will be saved. For with the heart one believes unto righteousness, and with the mouth confession is made unto salvation."

Imagine if a Christian sprinter were to have that moment in the camera after a big race, and she said something like this: "I just have a message for all you kids out there. You just really have to believe in God. And you have to believe in the Lord Jesus. Believe in your heart that God raised Him from the dead. Because then you will be free to run and train and work for His glory, and you will be free from the bondage of trying to save yourself or worship yourself. You will be free from thinking you have to create your own value or make your own dreams. Pursue Him, pursue His glory, and you will feel His pleasure."

Doesn't that sound shocking? Why? Because we have never heard anyone talk like that in public! You might think that I am taking what was always meant as shallow encouragement from the world and making a big deal about it. But what they say in those little sound bites is often as deep as it goes for them. The world has switched out the depth and richness and glory of believing entirely in another for your salvation, and they have replaced it with lame attempts at self-worship and self-identity. This is the philosophical version of carob chips, only a thousand times less satisfying. Total trust, total belief, total hope can only ever hang on one man, Jesus Christ, the Son of God. Believe entirely on Him, and you will be saved.

The world's effort to catechize us into believing in ourselves has caused much of our current identity crisis. If I am so obligated to believe in myself, then I ought to figure out who that is. Indecision and lack of ambition are poor qualities for the foundation of a belief system, but what if those things characterize me? Because right now I am not actually sure. If believing in myself is the path to success and fulfillment, then I'd better do it, obviously. But what if I actually have no idea who I am? Well then, I will have to make it my all-consuming mission to find that out. Even worse than not knowing, what if I can see myself, and I don't like what I find? What then? I have to become something. I have to become *worthy*. I have to make this body be perfect. I have to get implants. I have to get all the self-help (or self-deception) books on the market and study, study, study. I have to buy all the latest *Cosmos*, because their think-tank that discovers new sex tips every month may have some tidbit of information that will transform me into a sex goddess worthy of worship. I have to lie to myself and believe that I am more important at the office than I am. It's like padding your own resumé that only you are reading. And thus, we see that believing in yourself is the ultimate path not to freedom, but a horrible bondage.

For the world, "Who am I?" is actually a much bigger question because it is the question of "Who is my god?" or "On whom do I pin my hopes of salvation?" For the world, you must find yourself so you can love yourself, believe in yourself, and worship yourself. The imaginary resolution to this problem is to fall in love with yourself and be at peace at last. But it never really happens in a lasting way. Maybe by believing in yourself, you will make it all the way to an Olympic gold medal. Then what? Does that kind of achievement really make a sort of peaceful ending for anyone? We know from their testimonies that it doesn't. They end up hanging all their hopes on something that they hope to achieve, they achieve it, and then they still feel the same. They have the same hunger to be something, to matter. The trophy on the shelf is never synonymous with "they lived happily ever after."

Because worshipers become like what they worship, following the world's advice will take you into a tornado of tail chasing–trying to find out who you are so you can worship yourself, all while becoming more and more of a sad and confused worshiper of a lost and feeble god. You'll be looking constantly to find yourself in the hope that somehow it will relieve the pressure of trying to worship what you can't really see and honor what you can never really know.

It is an awkward situation, always kneeling in front of the altar that you meant to be on. Which are you to be? The worshiper or the worshiped? It is a spiritual impossibility, but working to get people to try to find themselves and worship themselves is actually big business. The world offers therapy, advice books, and support groups, and promotes many false ways to self-actualization. Despite so many people buying into this, it is a miserable job. When they manage to kneel, they find the altar is empty, and when they manage to clamber up on the altar there are no worshipers. It is the most unsatisfying of all arrangements, a quest that can't ever really be fulfilled. The good news is that if you are a Christian, it is a quest you can walk away from. Your purpose is elsewhere. This right here? It's just the quicksand of unbelief.

16

UNCONCERNED

ONE OF THE MOST FUNDAMENTAL WAYS
that the Christian faith disrupts the questions
of philosophy about self and identity is actually
by bypassing the whole issue: who I am is not
actually my concern. It is far from my responsibility and life's work to create and curate myself. For the Christian, the question of "Who am
I?" is actually just another way of asking "Who
is He?"

The answer to that question has the glorious
advantage of not being in process. It is fixed. It

is permanent. Hebrews 13:8 says with finality, "Jesus Christ is the same yesterday, today, and forever." And again, in James 1, "Every good gift and every perfect gift is from above, and comes down from the Father of lights, *with whom there is no variation or shadow of turning*" (v. 17, my emphasis).

He does not change, but goodness, how *we* do! In Him is no shadow of variation, but we go through a great many phases of life. Oftentimes it is just that passing of one phase and the beginning of another that causes us to question everything and start seeking answers again. It is the change that catches us off guard and makes us wonder what is happening. How did I turn into an old lady? When did I pass all my childbearing years? How am I this old and not settled on a career? Why do I suddenly not know or recognize myself? Wasn't I going to do something else with my life?

But God is permanent. He is forever. He is unshaken, unbroken, and unchanging, though we may be shaken and broken and changed. He is not worried or flustered. He is not having a midlife crisis or wondering what He is for. The passage of time does not leave Him altered in any way. Those shadows of sunsets and morning sunrises come and go, and we grow older and different every minute. The shadow of turning is itself one of the most fixed realities in our lives. But Jesus Christ is perfect, worthy, sufficient, holy, and He will be so forever. And He is ours. There is no shadow of turning in Him. There is no time that God is older than He feels, or when He is surprised by the bags under His eyes or the pain in His back. He does not change. He is fixed, and we can be fixed in Him.

So when the "searching" question shifts from wanting to talk all about *me* to wanting to pursue the glory of our everlasting God, we find that every question has an answer. The answer is so much bigger than we are. The foolish question, "What is the essential me?" will only leave us in doubt.

We are not fixed in ourselves. We have shadows of turning. Did the essential you have a much more youthful figure? Did you settle into that eighteen-year-old body, not realizing it was only passing you by? Then you (the essential you!) are lost forever after having children or just growing quietly older. Did the essential you have a lot of time to spend on yourself? If so, then the people or the tasks that disrupt your schedule are doing far more than that.

They are separating you from yourself. Tearing you apart! How could you not resent that? They are destroying something that was precious to you. Something you need. Something without which *you* could not be.

Do you see how dangerous this thinking is? It is not a hypothetical philosophical question but an abundantly practical one—it is a misunderstanding that destroys lives. If you decide that you are, in your essential self, a carefree girl, then how will you deal with heavy burdens in life? You will believe that they are (literally) killing you. Heavy burdens are fundamentally opposed to who you are. You have to escape to live. You have to leave your burdensome kids or your husband—anything to find yourself. Just think about that for a moment. Self-rescue takes precedence over everything, because you have allowed yourself to believe that you are actually being murdered by your situation.

This is a very common story. It is a life-crisis that we are familiar with. But we don't often hear people identify it as a philosophical problem. It comes out in little short blurts. "I just can't live like this." "I feel lost." "I don't know what to do anymore." "I have to get out." "I don't know who I am anymore."

We hear the "can't," "feel," "don't know," but what we should be noticing is the "I." This person believes they know who they are, and that this situation they are in is inconsistent with their person. They believe that they know and understand their own potential and limitations so well that they are fit to make the decision. They (in their essence) cannot live anymore in such a (opposed to their essence) situation. They must sacrifice anything to protect their perceived self.

But do they actually know themselves this well and in this way? No. That is why the other side of such selfish stories are never happily ever after. They can't walk out on their children or their vows or their family and then find themself in a new Eden of happiness. They actually don't know much at all about themselves, about what they can do, about how they can live, or where they should be.

In contrast to this, a Christian who is pursuing the glory of God is not threatened by changes. Because we are becoming ourselves through responsive obedience to God, we do not need either ourselves or our situations to be settled, because our whole lives are fixed on God, and He will not change. He is our anchor, and as the glorious hymn says, "In every high and stormy gale, / My anchor holds within the veil." When God sends burdens, it does not separate us from Him or from ourselves. When He takes things away from us, He does not change. The more we honor Him in our trials, the more like Him we become. The more like Him we become, the more we become the person we were created to be. Instead of carrying a burden that focuses on knowledge of self, we shift the burden to knowledge of Christ. He is sufficient. I am not nor shall I ever be. He is faithful. He is perfect. He is capable. He is enough. And more than all these things together, the sweetest gift of all is that He has given Himself to us.

We cannot know the limits of our God, because there are none. We can rest—rest—in Him no matter the uncertainty of our own circumstances.

When we shift our focus in difficult situations from ourselves to God and His glory, what will change in us? First of all, we will not suddenly come to know ourselves in a fixed way. It isn't that we will receive an exhaustive owner's manual for the self. Instead we will be simply assuming ourselves as we reflect God. Do you see the difference? We are no longer looking at ourselves as though we are the destination and the creature that we must ultimately nourish. We will instead be assuming ourselves and seeking to serve God with our selves. Our very selves become the tools with which we strive to serve God. If God changes the tool in some way, we know it is so we can better glorify Him. This leaves us secure in change, confident that this is for our good and His glory. We know the hands that we are in.

The strangest thing happens when you orient yourself around God and His glory. You forget yourself! Your confidence in yourself improves radically. You are in your natural habitat here (wherever that is). You are perfect for here. You were made for this. When your purpose is oriented to glorifying and serving God, you are not worried about yourself anymore. God has equipped you perfectly to honor and glorify Him, and He will continue to do so. Keeping your eyes on Him will give you so much more insight into what you were made for. Philippians 1:6 says, "being confident of this very thing, that He who has begun a good work in you will complete it until the day of Jesus Christ."

If a good work was begun in you at your conversion (and it was), that good work is being continued. What is more, it will be completed. What was the poured concrete of your foundation will over time turn into the framing of the walls and the roofing and the finish work. But it is all the good work that your God has begun in you, and He will see it through. The fact that the phases look different is not a sign of God quitting at one thing and starting another, but rather a sign that He is continuing that which He started.

If you assume this, you will find that when you have a question about your self, it will be one with a real answer. "Does this glorify God?" That is a question that has a real answer. You will find yourself spending approximately zero time on questions like, "But who am I really?" and spending more time on things like, "What is my duty here? How can I glorify God in this phase of life?" These are the kinds of questions that are seeking (and finding) real answers.

This is not some kind of vague and theoretical question either. It is not some existential bone to gnaw on, where deep down inside you may find a nutrient if you pursue it long enough and are clever enough. This is an answer with a lot of life-sustaining meat on it. You will probably have so much on your plate to do right away that you will stop thinking about the question at all. The Christian life is a life that is brimming over with answers. And good news: we have all the answers that we will ever need if only we ask the right kind of questions.

17

BE MADE NEW

WE LIVE IN A TIME WHEN PEOPLE ARE putting so much effort into finding out who they are that personality tests are ever-present. You only need to answer a set of questions about yourself, and it will reveal who you really are! Supplement that test with a playlist of TED Talks to *really* unlock the mysteries of all of our greatest strengths. We want more information about ourselves, all the time. Tell me how to help myself recharge. Tell me how to reach my fullest potential. Tell me how much more intelligent I am than the other personality types. Tell me my strengths, teach me my magic. And of course, the ghost of Sartre is ever-present as well: many tests tell us our failings in order to propose a new way to "self-realize" or a way to make ourselves into what we want to be, a Christ-less alternative to sanctification.

Let's draw out one specific aspect of personality tests. If you have ever taken one, you know the kinds of questions they ask. Do you like to be the center of attention at a party? Are you often late? Do you want everyone to know who you are? Do you feel most energized when you are left to yourself to think? Do you prefer variety or routine?

Imagine personality test questions with more context provided. Imagine the whole situation was spelled out in detail, and it went something like this.

"You go to a party at a friend's house, and the room is full of very interesting and sparkling people. Do you make your way toward them and join in the most lively conversation, or do you talk to the girl who came up beside you and is being strangely needy while wanting to talk with you about something that does not interest you at all?"

I assume that many of you are like me—the answers to this question would vary quite widely based on how much you were behaving according to the flesh and how much according to the Spirit. In the flesh, I would want to get in on the most interesting conversation. In the Spirit, I would want to reach out to the lonely. Which is my true personality?

James writes what he wants for us:

> But be doers of the word, and not hearers only, deceiving yourselves. For if anyone is a hearer of the word and not a doer, he is like a man observing his natural face in a mirror; for he observes himself, goes away, and immediately forgets what kind of man he was. But he who looks into the perfect law of liberty and continues in it, and is not a forgetful hearer but a doer of the work, this one will be blessed in what he does. (James 1:22–25)

If you hear the word of God and do not do it, you are like someone who cannot remember what he looks like—even after looking in the mirror. But if you look into the word and obey it—you will know who you are. You don't forget. In this way, we see that obedience is the path to clear and true self-knowledge.

Here's the fascinating thing about this: the knowledge of who you are is connected *not* to revelation of that fact at some point (like the results of a personality test), but rather to obedience. This means going forward and acting on what you have learned. Acting on what you have seen in the Word of God is what changes us. In other words, we are not fixed. Obedience changes us so thoroughly that it changes our own knowledge of self. How could any personality test compete with that?

Think of some personality trait of yours that you consider a fact of life. Maybe you are short-tempered. Or perhaps you are overly emotive. Maybe you are always discouraged, or prone to being critical. Do you tend to stress out and get worried easily? What are these traits like when they are in the Spirit? When you look into the Word of God as it addresses this personality trait of yours, what do you learn? What happens when you obey what you find there? That trait is transformed. You are transformed. Your personality is transformed.

A short temper, when it is controlled in an act of obedience, is what? Long-suffering. An unsteady spirit, being obedient, is what? Steadfast. A discouraged person, in Christ and obedient, is what? A faithful person. A critical spirit, curbed by obedience, is what? A kind spirit.

Far from our personalities being like eye color (something you are born with and can't do anything about), our personalities are something that God gave us so that we would have something to put on the altar and offer to Him. So you love quiet and time to journal? There is something in your hands that you can give up. So you love being at the heart of the social scene around you? There is something tangible God has given you to lay down. Do you see how this works? We are naturally full of instincts and desires that are contrary to what God wants us doing. That means that those things are something to *obey with*, not something to obey around.

Let's say that you are naturally disposed to worry, and, right in the middle of an anxiety fest, you open your Bible to see this: "Be anxious for nothing, but in everything by prayer and supplication, with thanksgiving, let your requests be made known to God; and the peace of God, which surpasses all understanding, will guard your hearts and minds through Christ Jesus" (Phil. 4:6–7).

Now let's imagine that you apply the admonition from James and immediately obey. You pray and ask God to take your worry. You lift up your concerns with thanksgiving. What does this passage tell you will happen? The peace that passes understanding will set about you like a guard dog. You will be protected from yourself!

So here we can see a very straightforward way in which obedience to God transforms you.

Perhaps the greatest concern about the nature of the personality test culture is that it comes at us looking to categorize us. Personality testers want to find the slot to put that trait in. They want to say, "Let me explain about you," but somehow what they discover is never anchored in the Word of God. And why would it be?

But the Christian should know better than this. God created you specifically with specific plans for what He was going to do with and through you. Some of what the world would call your essential traits, God would call kindling for the fire on His altar. Far from being your essential traits, they are just the chips coming off the block of marble as God shapes you into what He intends you to be.

We can let the strangest assumptions sneak in. We think that God created us in a sort of burst of creativity and after that it is all on us. But when we think that way, we are forgetting that every single breath, heartbeat, and thought, every act of cellular replication from each of the trillions of cells in our body, is a continued act of God upholding His creations. We are sustained in Him. God does not make us once and then let us go until the batteries run out.

Romans 11:36 says this: "For of Him and through Him and to Him *are* all things, to whom *be* glory forever. Amen."

Think on that! Say this to yourself: "I am of Him, I am through Him, and I am to Him. To Him be glory forever and amen!"

The great temptation is to start categorizing yourself outside of Him. What if I tried this with those categories going? "I am of the ENTJ branch of Him; I am energized by connections with other people, and my strengths are efficiency and energetic leadership, I am strong-willed and think strategically, and through those things I try to honor God when I get the chance, as I can, as my situation allows me to thrive, to whom be glory forever, amen."

Something got a little off here, didn't it? We are trying to define ourselves by categories that get between us and Christ. The reality is that we are continually being shaped, grown, changed, and used as we abide in Him. Of Him, through Him, to Him. That's what we are, and that is more than enough.

When we get distracted by looking at ourselves, we can start seeing things that are *simple* acts of obedience as tremendous sacrifices. *Because I am an introvert, this call to hospitality means that I am basically having to be superhuman. Because I love silence, receiving the gift of children is a tremendous spiritual sacrifice—one that I will suffer through (with a lot of complaining). Because I am such a dynamic leader (and my husband is not), it is really hard for me not to be in charge of everything, as I am naturally better at it.*

These sorts of things are not the truly superb sacrifices of an introvert or extrovert or leader, or whatever number or letter combination you have found yourself to be. It is the *normal* obedience of a *normal* Christian. God leaves none of His children empty handed. We all have something to give Him. Lay it down, and learn who you really are. Forget the numbers, learn what you need to know as you obey the Word.

If we are of Him and through Him and to Him, then we are being changed in obedience. Forget yourself. What is He like? He loves children. He wants us to be hospitable. If we are abiding in Him, it is not our preferences, but His preferences that define us. We are not the same people we were before obedience, *and we shouldn't want to be.*

We are not even being refined in accord with our personality types. It isn't as though a life of faithful Christian living will lead you gradually to be an opposite personality type, or to an ultimate Christian personality type. You are not a certain personality type becoming a different one, but rather an obedient or disobedient Christian becoming more obedient or less obedient. More Christlike or less Christlike.

What is even more important is that the same One who made us is the One who tells us how to obey. He knows what He is asking, and He knows what effect it will have on our lives, and He knows how it will feel to us. He knows we will have to lay down all our petty instincts and natural inclinations to live a spiritual life. He knows! And He tells us to do it because *He loves us.* Obedience is not wasted on Him or lost on Him. We can have complete confidence that if we live a life given to Him in this way—in a million small acts of obedience—*we are safe.*

18

MISUNDERSTOOD
PRINCESS

ALONG WITH A DESIRE TO STUDY OUR-
selves intensely comes the desire to treasure
ourselves. If you are a Christian woman who
has been in Christian circles at all, you have
no doubt been told that you are a princess. As
a daughter of the King, you are living a very
privileged life, and you are very precious and
beautiful, and you probably have a glass slipper
somewhere that has been overlooked.

I find this whole idea very unsatisfactory, and here is why. The underlying problem with this is that we are far removed from biblical ideas about royalty. It is not at all untrue that you are a daughter of the King. The King of the whole earth even. Amen! You are.

We have misused this truth to the point that it seems common to attribute to God all of the characteristics of the world's most indulgent father of a spoiled child at a mini-mall. We think a princess means having your nails done, tiaras, plastic high heels, and getting everything you ever wanted because your father doesn't know how to say no to you. He is a king, after all! He can buy me all the stuff I ever wanted. I shall go forth and demand it all. There might be small fluffy dogs in rhinestone bedazzled carriers, and you might even live in some kind of over-blown Barbie mansion.

So, what kind of a king is He? In reality, your Father is not a petty, child-indulging king—not at all what the princess encouragement makes Him out to be. We are quick to see the role of princess as one that has a lot of privilege in it, and it is in fact a privileged position. But more than that, it is a position of responsibility. You are a daughter of the King. That means you should be about His business. You are a daughter of the King—therefore bear your responsibilities in a way that becomes the office you hold. While it is a great honor, being a daughter of the King is more like wearing a shirt that says STAFF boldly across the back. When it comes to Kingdom work, we are the Kingdom workers. Who should be more invested in this work than the children of the King himself?

This brings us to the very heart of the matter: what is the nature of this kingdom, and how is it built? Look at the example of your Father. He sent His Son to lay down His life for His people. You belong, body and soul, to the kind of King who is building His kingdom on the mercy of self-sacrifice.

We are in the glorious position of following in our older brother's footsteps. God incarnate, Jesus Christ, is the author and finisher of our faith. When we look to Him, we see a glorious picture of what it means to be a child of God.

"For it was fitting for Him, for whom *are* all things and by whom *are* all things, in bringing many sons to glory, to make the captain of their salvation perfect through sufferings" (Heb. 2:10).

This passage makes it clear what the standard in this royal family is, and it is not self-indulgence. Here we have our first among many brethren, and what is the perfect example that He gives us? Laying down His life. Being perfected in suffering. Bringing us to glory.

The role of the child of God is a royal office. And as such it means that every Christian is called to lay down his life. We are called to live in imitation of our high priest and the selfless work that He accomplished for us. Romans 8 tells us that Jesus was the firstborn among many brethren, and for this reason, we can know that all things will work together for our good. We have been called according to His purpose. Do you see that? Our calling is His purpose. And what are we always on our way to doing? Becoming more like Jesus. "And we know that all things work together for good to those who love God, to those who are the called according to His purpose. For whom He foreknew, He also predestined to be conformed to the image of His Son, that He might be the firstborn among many brethren" (Rom. 8:28-29).

So, yes, I believe that you are royalty. You are a daughter of the Most High King, and you are a princess. But what does that mean practically? When this phrase is trotted out, it almost always comes off as addressed to someone looking hopelessly out of a window, wondering who they are while curled up in an afghan watching the rain drops on the window. It is a message for our feelings, intended to bolster us up in our needy moments. "No matter what you feel like, you are important. Feel spoiled. You are *super* important."

But, as we have established, we haven't been called to "feel awesome about ourselves"; we have been called to faithfulness. We have been called to His purposes. The reality of following Christ is not that kind of cheap affirmation. It is not an emotional Snuggie for our cold hearts. It is a different thing altogether. It is a cross being carried.

The moment where you can truly see the royalty of a Christian is in the middle of an impossible task or a heartbreaking need. It is a child of God looking at a trial and saying, "This is mine to handle. Let me do this for you. Let me hold the hand of the dying, let me care for the drug-addicted foster child, spend my life in a third-world country sharing the Gospel, mop the same floor I mopped yesterday and every day before that, or freely give away my time in a million ways with no expectation of getting it back. Let me change your diapers and hold your hand. Let me feed the hungry, and reach out to the lonely. *Let me.* I see my name all over this job. This is work for a daughter of the King."

A life of Christian royalty is not an easy one. It is full of trials and obstacles and suffering and troubles. Not only do we *endure* trials and suffering, we are called to turn those very things into blessings for others. How many ministries in this world have been started by people who went through something awful themselves and found both a gaping need and their own ability to do something about it? How many Christians have turned pain in their life into comfort for others? Every time you've read a testimony, you have heard a person acting like a child of the King. A person telling you how their cancer pointed them to Christ, how their darkest moments showed the kindness of the Father.

This is the duty of sons and daughters of the King. To lay down their lives for those around them. To point to Christ continually by imitating Him. To seek to live for His purposes and to trust Him that *all things*—all our trials and our sacrifices and our efforts in and around them—are going to work together for our good. Our identity in Christ is more about our responsibilities than about our privileges, though there will be many of those. Jesus Christ endured much for us—but now He is seated at the right hand of God the Father. We do not fear because we know a time of perfect rest, a time of glory, a time of perfect happiness will come—but that time is not yet and our work is not done. Work hard in the hope of that glory, and "endure hardship as a good soldier of Jesus Christ" (2 Tim. 2:3).

19

YOUR FAMILY TREE

MY GRANDFATHER IS IN HIS NINETIES now and has been a faithful and diligent evangelist for many, many years. He loves to give away missionary biographies, and because of his love for them and his love for giving them away, I read many as a child. My children read them often now, raking in a new load every time Grandpa Jim brings a box of books to our family dinner. Occasionally I grab one off the shelf and reread it, revisiting a literary genre that has shaped me in more ways than I know.

When I read them as a child, I was simply reading an adventure story. They were exciting! There was lots to be interested in or thrilled by: encounters with witch doctors, the terrifying excitement of smuggling Bibles into a country, hiding Jews in secret rooms—they were all good stories just by themselves. But now when I read them, their stories strike me in a totally different and overwhelming way.

I am in a completely different world than these heroes of the faith were. I am not in the same time period, not from the same church background, not even from the same theological persuasion much of the time. None of the things in the stories are about me or my life, save one: my Father is in those stories. When I read about His tender love and care of His children, I learn more about Him. When I read how He used His children from all over the world for His purposes (those accidental meetings of saints that were obviously perfectly coordinated, the answers to prayer that involve complicated answers to multiple prayers all coming from different directions), then I see how our Father loves all His children with such attention and faithfulness. He provides for their every need, answers their prayers when they didn't believe it was possible, introduces them to each other when they could not have found each other by any other means. When I rejoice in His love for them, I rejoice in His love for me. When I love those He loved, I learn more about who He is. And more than that, when I read about the trials and obstacles that our brothers and sisters in Christ experience, through them I learn about myself, too. Because when you learn about the way in which God upholds His people when they go through trials trusting in Him, and when they rely on Him for their every need, you are also learning about your own trials and your own needs. You are learning about your family, your Father, and yourself all at once. You are learning about another part of the body that you belong to.

We live in an age that has a deep love of the individual, but we are a lonely and disconnected people, trying to find out who we are. But when you know that you are part of the body of Christ, you can easily look around you to see who you are. This is you. The body of Christ is all over and it is manifestly knowable. There is no shortage of information. There is more here to find out than you can absorb in a lifetime.

When I read an account of Bible smugglers, I read about my own love for God's Word. Tears roll down my cheeks as I read about tears rolling down the cheeks of an old man getting his own Bible for the first time. I am part of him and he is part of me. When I read about preachers who preached at night in the woods to people who knew they might die for gathering, I read about their strength and think about what I will do to hear the Word preached. These are my people. This is who I am.

Some people might be thinking that it is a little bit presumptuous to read stories of other people's virtues and treat them as your own. And of course I am not confusing my own life and actions with theirs. But that reaction is missing the heavy, rich, amazing truth that is here. I am not reading their virtues as mine, I am accepting *their* Christ as *my* Christ. The Spirit who was in them is in me. His holiness was their holiness, His strength their strength. I am accepting that what He has done in others He can do in me. What I see in their stories of living for Christ is Christ's holiness, His kindness, His provision for them as they burned at the stake, as they refused to recant, as they stood in the face of impossible opposition and loved Him. This is learning about me because it is learning about the One in whom I live—the One in whom they lived on earth and in whom they still live in Heaven.

We aren't simply a bunch of isolated individuals. Corporately, we are the bride of Christ. Corporately, we are one. Different parts of the body have different gifts and abilities and callings, but we are still one in Him.

"For as the body is one and has many members, but all the members of that one body, being many, are one body, so also is Christ. For by one Spirit we were all baptized into one body—whether Jews or Greeks, whether slaves or free—and have all been made to drink into one Spirit. For in fact the body is not one member but many" (1 Cor. 12:12–14).

If you are needing to know who you are, you can take a simple step toward finding out and study faithful believers. You can read about them, you can go talk to other Christians, you can listen to them preach. It is not nearly as hard as it may seem to gather information about yourself. Objective, glorious, encouraging, faith-building information. There are big stories and there are anecdotes, famous heroes and people who have no books about them but who walk through the story with so much grace and glory.

Recently I thought to ask my grandpa why he liked missionary biographies so much. It was such a part of him that I hadn't even noticed that it isn't exactly normal behavior.

He told me that when he was first saved, in his twenties at the Naval Academy, he hadn't known any Christians. He didn't know how he would learn to behave like a Christian. He had no one to imitate, no idea how to do it, and no idea who to look to. Then it struck him that he could still imitate Christians who were dead. They didn't have to be people you knew in real life for you to become like them. Thus began his lifelong ministry and enjoyment of biographies of great Christians. They were his mentors and his encouragement. They were his explanations of how prayer works and who God is. Through them he understood himself and what he belonged to. Saints gone on before us are still ministering to us here through records of their faithfulness.

I think my grandpa was on to something all those years ago. If you want to know who you are and how to be you, get to know *your people*. Read about them. Read about their anxieties and their answers to prayer. Read about their courage that came not from themselves but from God. There is so much to know about your people that you won't even scratch the surface of your own inheritance in the faith. Look into the books like you are reading your own story—one that will actually tell you the truth about God and leave you knowing more about yourself.

This is the spiritual version of taking a DNA test and finding out you are descended from royalty. You don't turn from that discovery and say that your ancestors are of no interest to you, but rather, "Now I know how important I am!" You do not go sit down in front of a mirror to find out the "real" info about yourself. Maybe make some sketches of your own hands to find out who you are. Maybe do some close-up study of your eyes. The longer you gaze at yourself, the less you really know. If you think being royalty is located in your pores and not in your family history, you are kidding yourself. This information about you is not inside you but outside you. It is the same with your heritage in the faith. Look behind you and beside you for the things God is doing in you and for you. Your Christian brothers and sisters have stories, and all those stories have one Giver. Love Him, love them, and be shaped.

There is a tremendous amount of information available about who you are and where you belong. It's not even hard to get at. All you need to do is run into my Grandpa Jim, and he'll be more than happy to give you something to get you started.

20

LIKE SO MANY MONKEYS

SAMUEL RUTHERFORD PENNED THIS gem: "Your heart is not the compass Christ saileth by."

What a glorious thought that is! Christ is not subject to the insights or the whims of our hearts. And while we might feel that our hearts produce nothing but the most valuable insights, Rutherford might say, "Christ regardeth them not."

Why is this such a humbling truth? Because in spite of the fact that we want to admire them, our hearts—our innermost insights—are fickle.

They do not point to the truth. Our hearts have, in fact, gone so far away from truth-telling that it is safe to call them liars. The Bible never tells us to trust ourselves, believe ourselves, listen to ourselves. Jeremiah 17:9 is a famous passage that is nowhere near famous enough. "The heart is deceitful above all things and beyond cure. Who can understand it?" (NIV).

We are accustomed in our times to think of our feelings as information. We believe that when we feel something, it is not only revealing an actual thing that is going on, but probably insightful about what ought to go on.

A woman "feels" unwanted and unloved, so she accuses all those who want and love her of creating her feelings. A Christian may "feel" like God isn't close, and so he continues to disobey Him or avoid praying. We "feel" like we really need a break right now, and so we take one, whether or not our duties and responsibilities allow for it.

We Christians need to stop thinking of our feelings as insights. Our feelings are instead something that we need to manage. When our feelings are acting up, who is to discipline them? We are. Who is to treat them with reverence? No one.

Now to bring this full circle: I hope that you see the reason we admire and esteem our feelings is because we believe that, under the surface of our lives and actions, there lies an essential *us*. The real self, sometimes buried under all our daily activities, is in there somewhere. And we think that when we get a feeling out of the clear blue sky, it must be an important message from the most important person of all—us. We assume that with unerring insight our true self has deemed it necessary to communicate, and of course we should not only listen to it, but immediately share the news with all those around us. This feeling, generated from within us where the "self" is, must be true. It must be the thing we all need to hear, acknowledge, respect, and obey.

But Christians should be far more inclined to view our feelings like a bunch of monkeys that we are responsible to keep in cages, train, and disregard completely when they are acting up.

Scripture is full of admonitions to the emotions. Think of the psalms and their many admonitions to the self: O my soul, why are you grieving? Why are you cast down, O my soul? Why are you disquieted within me? (c.f. Ps. 42:5). The psalmist acknowledges his various feelings, but he does so to counsel himself, not to wallow in the situation. He finishes all those acknowledgments of his emotions with calls to obedience. Hope in God! Praise Him! He is your helper, your salvation. He sustains you. He will vindicate you. In other words, the psalmist takes the emotional impulses that he has and turns them into remembering God, trusting in God, praising God, hoping in God.

If our feelings are like a bunch of monkeys, then we live in a world full of people trying to follow their unleashed monkeys through life. This monkey is bound to know the way! We are told over and over (and over) that you must (must!) follow your heart. And what our society has reaped from that unerring pursuit has been exactly what you might expect: a lot of wildly undisciplined and confused people, anxiously following their own wildest ideas, doing every self-indulgent and ill-behaved thing they can think of. We make the monkeys in the real monkey houses blush for us.

Let's say you agree with the prophet Jeremiah that your heart is a terrible guide. So then, think about your own feelings. Think about the specific ones you have let define you. You have listened to them as though they are the bulletin from the inner Holy of Holies. You have respected the fountain of information within. Perhaps you have learned from yourself that you are unwanted because you feel unwanted. Maybe you believe that you are needy because you feel needy. Maybe you believe that you are taken for granted because you feel taken for granted. Maybe you believe that you are shameful because you still feel shame for some past sin. Maybe you believe that you are lonely because you feel lonely.

Next, I want you to take that particular monkey—that identity feeling—and ask the Lord what He thinks of it. And I will guarantee you that what He thinks is not what you think. He does not agree with the leadership of that monkey.

This is what brings us to the daily crux of a Christian's personal holiness: you are commanded to act like what you believe to be true is actually true. Your feelings tell lies; deal with it. Your innermost thoughts and treasured emotions are probably deceitful little monkeys that are doing (faithfully, effectively, and diligently) the work of the enemy in your life. They are distracting you, they are leading you astray, they are wasting your time. If you are self-absorbed, wallowing around in how you feel, they may be winning.

But there is no need for the enemy to be winning in your daily life, because he has lost your eternal life. When you treat your feelings like a psychologist's report from your true (honest and faithful) self instead of distractions from your inner monkeys, you set yourself up for horrific idolatry. Because our feelings are often accusatory and ugly, we do not see the idolatry for what it is. If it is all flattery and admiration of self, we might not be as easily led astray. But it is often a more effective ploy of the enemy to accuse, to loathe, and to demean, to point fingers and set up comparisons. We fail to realize that, in trusting the self completely, we are worshiping the self. We are letting it usurp the place of God and His word in our lives. We believe self over Him. We listen to the self instead of listening to God. We choose the monkeys and all their shenanigans over Christ and His perfect leadership. We believe that the monkeys, however ugly they may be, are being honest.

What is the solution for a Christian who realizes he has been falling into this kind of identity disobedience? The answer is always Christ. Turn the whole monkey house over to Him, and ask Him to teach you the truth. Ask Him to lead you. Ask Him to show you what you ought to feel. Ask Him to show you how to live your emotional life as becomes a follower of Christ. Ask Him to teach you how to ignore your own feelings righteously when they are in the wrong, and to teach you how to make them obey. Ask Him to give you nerves of steel as you walk past the cages of the howling, disobedient, and ugly monkeys and follow Him. Your life cannot be built on the "leadership" of your emotions, if you want any of your endeavors or relationships to hold up.

What about the alternative? What about walking right past our feelings to follow Christ? Will we ever see our true selves? Will we ever have a right feeling? We are fond of the companionship of our feelings and would miss them! This is the amazing reality of following Christ: when we ignore our feelings, they follow. They can learn to obey, too. These ridiculous monkeys are terrible leaders but the most wonderful followers once they figure it out. It will take time and practice, and there will be many opportunities to fail and confess and start over and try again. But do not let this deter you from the goal of following Christ! Follow Him! Look to Him! Let your emotions die in Him and be resurrected in Him. Believe what He has told you—believe who you are in Him. You will not turn into some kind of robot who has no feelings. You will become a Christian whose feelings live with you as they were meant to—in accordance to God's Word.

21

BODY IMAGE

ONE AREA WHERE THE MONKEY HOUSE of emotions are often very busy acting up is in the area of body image. When the world speaks of body image, it is almost always in the context of poor body image. This includes feeling bad about our bodies, thinking we are unattractive, failing to have respect for what our bodies are doing for us, struggling with low self-esteem, and any other unhealthy habit with regard to how we view our bodies. We speak of body image as something that needs to be healed.

The thing about body image is that while it involves something very central to ourselves (our mind, our body), it is almost always shaped in relationship to others. We don't like the way we compare to our more attractive friends or the imaginary airbrushed women on the magazine cover being sold at the grocery store. We don't like ourselves, because we have not attracted attention in a way that other people have. Our life is not a barrage of flattery and longing looks from strangers. And so we turn to our bodies and accuse them. We hate our bodies. We remember times when our bodies were behaving better, and we could tolerate them, and we try to bring that memory up in a way that will shame our bodies. What a strange game.

The world is currently very concerned about poor body image, and it spends a great deal of time trying to get us all to embrace our own nudity without shame. Maybe if we got fatter underwear models it would help, they say. But the world only sees one side of the problem and not the other. For a Christian, self-love is just as much a body image trouble as is self-loathing. Our bodies are not made for hatred, and they are not made for worship. When you try to solve the problem of loathing by preaching the problem of love, what you will end up with is all disaster and no solutions. We need a solution for this that is well outside our own naturally sinful instincts.

If the problem is that no one is attracted to you, then the solution is certainly not to become attractive to yourself. When the problem is that all your friends are hotter, the solution is not to start seeking to out-hot them. When the problem is a failure to thank God for what He has given you, the solution is certainly not to start thanking yourself diligently.

Our bodies are so much more than we deserve, no matter what. In the hands of an almighty Creator, our hearts pump magical fluid full of needful things all over our bodies. Our lungs, in a constant state of rising and falling, load up that magic fluid with oxygen. Our hands can do many things, our eyes are equipped to see the world. The same eyes that we use to look longingly at others and resent the profound gifts that we have been given are themselves enormous gifts.

We stand in our bodies that are upheld entirely by the will of our God, and we fill our hearts with resentment and ingratitude. We

look in the mirror at a body that is a gift entirely beyond our comprehension, and say to ourselves, "I hate it, ughhh!"

Sometimes we don't like changes that have
taken place without our permission. Turns out
you can't be eighteen for more than a year. You
have to go on and do something with your body.
Sometimes profitable, and that leaves a mark.
Sometimes unprofitable, and that leaves a mark.
You might be getting smile lines or smoking
wrinkles, but we are all going to get something.
Sometimes we hate ourselves for what we have
become, trying to drown our anger with all the
guilt, hoping to somehow deal with it by dissecting every instance of overeating or indul-
gence in disgust. That never works either.

The world tells us with endless enthusiasm
that we can work our way to a perfect state
of accepting ourselves and loving ourselves.
The goal, they say, is to be able to love what
you see in the mirror. They tell us that by constantly working on our self-love techniques
and talking to ourselves we may arrive at a
state of peace. We may get there where we can
look at ourselves and say, "You are amazing!
I love you." But if we do get ourselves there,
what earthly good will it actually do us? It is

just the unfortunate work of trying to get your saggy, cellulite-bespeckled self mounted up as an idol. Even if you have managed to get your body into a chiseled and perfect shape, it's still a sad piece of work. No matter how many times you tell yourself you are fierce or looking hot, nothing will come of it. There is no salvation, no freedom here.

The Christian should have an entirely different set of goals and aspirations. To what end has our body been given to us? So that we might glorify God. Do you know something that glorifies God? Christians glorify God when they are able to look in the mirror at their bodies—with all their faults and flaws and foibles—and truly love the One who gave it to them. That is the measure of a healthy body image.

This body is not your own. It is on loan. It was given freely to you by the Great Giver, so who among us should dare to complain? Do you have a body? Praise Him. Do you have problems with your body? Thank Him, and then glorify Him in your cheerful work on it. Do you have weight to lose? Thank God for all the blessings that got you here, and glorify Him by learning self-control. Do you have health problems? Thank Him that you have a body at all. Thank Him for His

abundant mercies thus far and ask Him to glorify Himself in how you pursue healing.

A Christian woman who is glorifying God will
see that what she needs to be able to do is look
in the mirror and *love God*. Who knit you together in your mother's womb? Who formed you
and made your heart beat? Who gave you every
breath you have ever taken and every color you
have ever seen and everything you have ever felt
and every bite you have ever taken? Praise Him!

You don't need to love yourself, you need
to love your Maker! Who made your body capable of bearing life? Who made it stretch to
its fullest and leave behind the tiger stripes of
fruitfulness? Praise Him! Who gave you eyes to
see? Who gave you feet to stand on? Your God
did that. He did it for you. The only appropriate
response to these gifts you have been given is
to worship your God. When you are full of this
kind of gratitude and praise, do you think you
are also making ugly faces at yourself and pick-
ing at all your flaws every time you see yourself?

Body image problems are fundamentally relational, and that is why the solution to them
is fundamentally relational. Orient yourself to
your God. We are made in the image of God.
Who do you image? Do you have a bad body

image? Stop trying to image the fake women on billboards and turn instead to your God. Stop trying to image the imaginary woman you think you could be in the mirror and start trying to faithfully image your God. What does that look like?

It looks like someone who knows exactly who they are (God's) and what they are for (for God). When you know your Creator, and you seek to praise and reflect and honor Him in every way possible, what that looks like to the world is body confidence. Are you ashamed of the way that your Creator made you? Not when you are seeking to glorify Him. When you seek His glory, do you care that other people might not admire your figure? No, because you are at peace with your God—what possible reason could you have for caring what your neighbor thinks? Any flashes of discontent are quickly offered up to your God and reoriented to gratitude. He is then glorified in your body, in your orientation to your body, in your lack of concern about what someone else thinks, and in your faithfulness confessing sin. In this context, everything is working exactly as it should.

Now think with me for a minute—would a woman who could do that be a woman who was being less her true self or more? Think about it. Be honest. Would she be less confident in her body or more? Would she be more fun and interesting as a person or less fun and interesting? The result of this kind of freedom from self and freedom to joy is what the world is trying (through all their counterfeit strategies) to duplicate. You already have access to the real thing. Worship your God well, and you will live more fully and freely yourself.

22

TURN TO CHRIST

BEING ORIENTED TO CHRIST AND TO the glory of God is in fact the answer to almost every human trouble. The fact that it is almost always the correct answer is not the same thing as being the answer we always want to hear. The phrase "Turn to Christ" is a well-trod path in Christian encouragement. You have probably heard it before, and here I am saying it all over again. If you are struggling in your life, this kind of advice might make you feel like you are being dismissed.

Do you feel lonely? Turn to Christ. Do you feel like you are starving for answers? Turn to Christ. Do you feel like you are laboring under burdens that are destroying you? Turn to Christ. Do you feel the deep need to know and be known? Turn to Christ. Do you wonder where the time is going and why anything matters? Turn to Christ.

I know that for many of you this admonition would make you think something like this: "Yes, yes, I see Christ. But what about this mess here? I'm talking about this mess in my life, I am not talking about Him! I know He is perfect, I just can't figure out how that is supposed to help me right now! I want to be known because I want a husband, not because I don't know about Christ. I want to be free of the guilt and shame of my weight problem because I want to be attractive, and I don't see how looking to Christ will magically make me more appealing! I want someone to tell me that I matter to them and that I am important, not read the words of Christ because He says those things to everyone. I want something more than that. Stop telling me to look to Christ because I already know about Him and I'm still here having this problem!"

This reveals something that is wrong in our thinking. Jesus Christ is not a glorious mountain that makes up part of the scenery of our life. Looking at Him in the distance as though He was an immobile and indifferent thing is part of the problem. We think we are looking to Christ when what we are doing is simply being aware of His existence. We know that will not help our problems because we are aware of His existence, and we were aware of His existence back when we got into this trouble in the first place.

Imagine that the moon was having a hard time. Imagine it crying to itself, saying, "I don't know what to do anymore! I don't feel useful. I don't feel beautiful. I just sit here in the darkness all the time with no purpose, no goals, no identity. I feel useless, adrift. No one cares about me or wants me to be anything special." What if someone could say to the moon, "Look to the sun! Just do what you were made for! Reflect the glory! Look to the sun while you go on your journey and your face will be bright! You are beautiful when you are oriented to the sun. You are purposeful when you are oriented to the sun. You are needed when you are oriented to the sun. You were made to be oriented to the sun!" Now imagine the moon saying something like, "Oh, that? That seems sort of unrelated. Why would that help me? What does that have to do with anything? I mean, I know it is there, but it has always been there. It doesn't have anything to do with the way I am feeling right now. It just seems like pointless platitudes. It doesn't really feel like you are listening to me."

On a fundamental level, we were created in order to do this. This is our purpose. This is our calling. Whenever we are feeling lost and adrift and without purpose or goals or people who want us, we are in the middle of not doing our most fundamental job of looking to Christ. We don't look to Him like we are looking at a postcard of a faraway place. We do not look to Him like He is a piece of information in a textbook. We do not look at Him like we look at an old family snapshot, remembering a good time. We look to Him as we were created to look to Him—in an interactive, glorifying relationship. We reflect His glory. This metaphor of the moon and the sun is a biblically accurate metaphor for our relationship to Christ. Look at this passage in 2 Corinthians: "But whenever anyone turns to the Lord, the veil is taken away. Now the Lord is the Spirit, and where the Spirit of the

Lord is, there is freedom. And we all, who with unveiled faces contemplate the Lord's glory, are being transformed into his image with ever-increasing glory, which comes from the Lord, who is the Spirit" (3:17–19, NIV).

Do you see how much this tells us about what our orientation ought to be? About what it means to look to Christ? To be oriented to Him? Do you see the purpose and the calling here? Would you like to be transformed into His image with an ever-increasing glory? Would you like to be free? Because here we are being called to freedom and to glory—and what does it take for us to get there? It takes us turning to Christ as we contemplate the Lord's glory. We look to Christ. We live to Christ. We live to Him, and consequently we can live in a state of ever-increasing glory. Who among us would ever say we didn't really want that? Would we prefer a stagnant life of bondage to a life of forever increasing, glorifying freedom?

This is what is offered to us. Be what you were created to be. Live in freedom. Live in a state of looking on glory and becoming glory. Could you ask for anything more? And if you want that but you don't feel you are doing it for some reason, the right answer really is "turn to

Christ." See your Savior. Orient your life to Him. Turn to Him completely.

We cannot stop the change that takes place in our lives just as the moon cannot stop her own motion. She is turning, she is moving, and yet she is focused on the sun and remains so through all her many seasons of change. And so, like her, should we. As we face our Savior through all our days, glorifying Him and receiving His glory in us, our changes and our turning only make the glory more pronounced. We submit to His will for seasons in our life, we reflect His glory through all of them in our own varying capacities. This is our purpose. This is our glory, and this is our ultimate freedom.

STUCK

AT THE TIME I AM WRITING THIS BOOK, MY youngest son is two, full of plans and hilarity and all that makes two such a fabulous age. It is that perfect age where they have a strong will but a toddler understanding—which makes for so many comedy sketches of human nature. He does in his small way what all of us do in our more complicated ways. He doesn't hide the journeys of the human heart—he lives them out in a comedy skit.

The other day he walked behind our couch (which is angled slightly away from the wall), jamming himself all the way into the corner with his head pinned between the couch and the wall and then began fussing that I needed to move the couch. "I'm stuck! My head is stuck!"

Now, I knew that his head was not stuck because when I didn't come running right away, he turned around to check why I hadn't, and on seeing me approach, quickly stuck his head back in the wedge, bemoaning the situation of heads stuck against difficult furniture arrangements. Why don't you move this couch, Mom? Don't you care for me? Can't you see that I have no choice but to press forward into this tiny, skull-crushing crevice? This is an impossible situation! The wall is unyielding! The couch will not move! Intervene, lest I die!

Of course I did not move the couch. There was nothing about the couch that was causing toddlers to get their heads stuck. I told him to take a step backward and turn around. "You aren't stuck! You are just going the wrong way."

I said it was a human nature comedy sketch, and it certainly is. How many of us have spent valuable time in just such spiritual situations? God's law won't move. Reality won't change. But I want to go this way and it is crushing me. I want to press myself hard into a place with no trajectory. I want to follow my sin and not God's path. I want to stuff myself into a corner and fuss at everyone else for not accommodating my plan. Or maybe just my mood. Or maybe my personal identity.

Right now, as a culture, we are facing a movement of people with their heads stuffed behind couches. They believe it is everyone else's fault that things are not comfortable for them. Their heads are stuck. Their hearts cannot comply with a simple command to turn around and walk out to the right way. This cannot be a dead end because I am here. My will is here. My plan is here. Therefore, it must be the way. It must be the truth. It must be the life.

But the way of sin is never the right way. There is no freedom, there is no greater understanding, and it will not make your life more fun or more fulfilling or more interesting in the long run.

Why are humans so easily tempted into this kind of thinking? If it isn't the way of anything good, what keeps us going there? When you rummage into a sin corner like this one, you feel like you are still being brave and independent. Even after it ceases to feel free or fun anymore, at least you are being "yourself." At least you still have your own will.

We instinctively believe that the pursuit of our own will is self-enriching. We assume that following ourselves into the tight corner will bring our true selves up to the surface. Even if we know this might be the wrong path, surely, we tell ourselves, it will be full of good findings, like a path through a fascinating forest with lots of opportunity for growth and discovery, with beautiful vistas and breathtaking flora and fauna. Self-actualizing at its most beautiful!

But of course that is not the case. Sin diminishes and destroys the self. Worshiping and serving the creature instead of the Creator never causes growth or spiritual progress. Worshiping the self drives it further into full-throttled self-destruct mode. Far from enhancing our own will, sin minimizes it. When we push ourselves into a corner, thinking that at least we are our true selves there, we are cut off from the very source of our true selves—our Creator. The true self requires others and can't be found in isolation.

Romans 1:20–23 is a very well-known passage that clearly spells out this situation:

...So that they are without excuse, because, although they knew God, they did not glorify Him
as God, nor were thankful, but became futile in
their thoughts, and their foolish hearts were
darkened. Professing to be wise, they became
fools, and changed the glory of the incorruptible God into an image made like corruptible
man—and birds and four-footed animals and
creeping things.

The fallen, sinful human heart wants to
change the creational order and turn it on its
head to glorify self rather than God. Once this
is accomplished, there is no need to thank God
because, after all, what has He really done for
you? It was you, was it not, who chose this
path? Why would you thank Him for your own
choices?

Scripture explains the consequences of this.
Your thinking will become futile. Your foolish
heart will be darkened. You become foolish in
the pursuit of self-wisdom, and exchange the
glory of God for an image that is made like corruptible man or beasts or insects.

In other words, when man turns from God to
worship the self (remember, this means to follow and obey the self), he turns away from being

the image of incorruptible glory. He loses the glory that he was made to reflect. When oriented correctly to God, we image His never-failing glory. When man severs himself from a posture of thanksgiving to God, he severs himself from the immediate fruit of that gratitude, which is wisdom. When a man stops giving thanks, he becomes a fool.

We must realize that the pursuit of the self has absolutely nothing in its favor. If you turn away from God, you have turned away from your best self. You have turned away from your glory, you have turned away from your wisdom, and you have turned away from fulfillment.

And yet, even in a culture like ours where dark-hearted foolishness seems to be everywhere, there is still good news. There is a good path. There is a good way. It's not too late to turn to God, glorify Him as God, and give Him thanks. Whether the corner you have pushed yourself into is a corner of small and petty grievances that have made the duties and relationships surrounding you feel impossible, or whether the corner is far more fundamental to your perception of yourself, there is always hope. Turn back to God. Glorify Him. Not as some kind of a helper for you, or as an emotional support.

Glorify Him as *God*, as the One who spoke you from nothing. Glorify Him as the One who told you not to go behind the couch and get your head stuck in the corner. Glorify Him with your obedience, with your turning, with your gratitude, with your new-found freedom as you walk on the only true path.

Glorify Him by thanking Him and growing wise. Glorify Him with your *self*. With all of it.

24

BEIGE AND BORING

WE DON'T WANT TO BE LIKE JESUS BE-
cause we like plain old us better. We value what
we see as our uniqueness apart from Him. On
some level, we are all tempted to believe that
we ourselves, even in our sin, are more interesting than we would be in Christ.

We fall into the ridiculous assumption that
being in Christ will be, in some way, flat; that we
will all be beige and wear beige and have nothing interesting to talk about, because we will

all be flattened into one big, undifferentiated, Christian blob of humanity.

On the one hand, this is what reveals our darkest bit of idolatry—our desire to cling to Me, *no matter what*. Rather me in sin than Him in me. This is ultimately hell: being left to ourselves and our desires, and being given free reign.

On the other hand, this fear reveals our lame imaginations. Do we really believe that our God, who created this exotic, varied, beautiful, and colorful world, is actually, deep down inside, boring? Do we think that we, the creatures He spoke into existence, are somehow more fascinating than the One who thought of us? If we do what He says, will we become less than He made us to be? We want to honor the creature and snub the Creator. We want to believe that He is not as clever as we are and His ideas are not as interesting as ours would be, if only we could get our hands on the steering wheel.

We see this kind of assumption, for example, when we Christian women believe that obeying Christ and submitting to our own husbands is going to somehow make us less than we are. It is going to take our will and smash it and ruin it and make us small and one dimensional, and

BEIGE AND BORING 211

less us. But this is the total opposite of the truth. Obedience to God always, always, beautifies. It always adds dimension and fullness, which are the results of living how we were meant to live. Our greatest potential will be found in our greatest obedience. We will not be losing ourselves in obedience but gaining our *true* selves. God is the One with the blueprints after all. We think that obedience is going to give us the short shrift, but it is actually the plan for our success and thriving. Obedience will not flatten us.

I hope you have had the pleasure of reading *The Hiding Place* by Corrie Ten Boom. It tells the story of Corrie and her sister Betsie through imprisonment in Holland and Germany during WWII—their trials, their faith, their loss, their tears, their joy. It is an overwhelming story. Through it all is Corrie, clinging to Christ, being conformed into His image, and being sanctified. When you close that book, you would never, ever say, "It would have been an amazing story if only I could have seen more of Corrie and less of Christ."

It sounds ludicrous, doesn't it? Corrie is such a vibrant character—certainly not made less vibrant by her reliance on her Savior. She is lovely and interesting and faithful and fierce. She is certainly worth reading about because she is in a constant state of laying herself on the altar for Christ. She is hardly the flat, one-dimensional person that we imagine we would become if we submitted totally to God. And Corrie would not have been a richer character if she had rejected Christ and embraced bitterness and hate.

Romans 8 lays this out for us in a most glorious passage:

> And we know that all things work together for good to those who love God, to those who are the called according to His purpose. For whom He foreknew, He also predestined to be conformed to the image of His Son, that He might be the firstborn among many brethren. Moreover whom He predestined, these He also called; whom He called, these He also justified; and whom He justified, these He also glorified. (vv. 28-30)

Look at the second sentence: to what have we been called? Being conformed to the image of His Son, the firstborn among many brethren. If you have been called according to His purpose,

BEIGE AND BORING   213

then you are being glorified into the image of His Son. To be conformed to Him is to be *glorified.*

Jesus Christ, our older brother, is so much more than we are that we have to be *glorified* in order to be conformed into His image. Far from getting flattened into a beige brick mold, we are being glorified through all manner of means into something consistent with our older brother. We are being conformed, but it is being conformed *into an everlasting glory.* This is not a bad bargain. Let go of your garbage and take His glory.

Your ultimate options are to be in your self-made costume in Hell, or in your real self, re-made in Christ and in Heaven. Whatever precious things you cherish in yourself apart from Christ must be surrendered willingly so they can be raised and glorified in Christ. Ask yourself if you want them in Hell. Because that is the only place that you can have them as they are. But if you give them up willingly, in Christ they will be raised. They will be glorified.

Maybe you shy away from this kind of talk because it sounds like you might be getting swallowed up. What happened to you? Where has all of your individuality gone? This might sound boring for all of us to be like Christ, but is it really?

Romans 10:9 says that "if you confess with your mouth the Lord Jesus and believe in your heart that God has raised Him from the dead, you will be saved."

What will be saved? *You.* What will no longer be lost? *You.* You aren't just a little tally somewhere of one more unit of humanity that will now be in Heaven eternally—one more beige brick of boring obedience. Jesus Christ came to save you specifically, and in Him, your Creator-Savior-King, you are free to be fully yourself.

If this is such good news, what possible reasons could we have for resisting it? Why is this not the most popular message to Christians everywhere? *Stop trying to be true to yourselves, people! Hell is full of the true-to-self crowd! Be true to Christ! Let it all go! You are in good hands! It is far sweeter, more fun, and more interesting to die in Christ than to live to the self.*

Why isn't this the subject matter of inspirational greeting cards and calendars? There's really no other answer than the one we've been discussing: because, in the flesh, we don't want it.

When I was a child, I got a pair of roller skates. I was skating in the kitchen, and my older sister by four years gave me some tips. My mom said something like, "Rachel, isn't it nice to have an older sister who can help you learn how to do something new?"

And I, in all of my fleshiest flesh, said something outraged like, "No! I did it all by myself!"

We hate the idea of not getting the glory for our best selves. We would prefer the glory. We think, "This was probably my doing anyway." Although my older sister gave me tips, I was magical on my own. What I received was unnecessary.

And this brings me to the hardest part of this book. Nonetheless, I believe it is the most important.

Here it is: as Christian women, we have to look directly at our salvation in an honest manner. We have to see, acknowledge, believe, and rejoice over the death of self.

25

DEATH OF SELF

I HAVE SAID THAT WE MUST LOOK AT our salvation head on. We must be willing to see what that transaction actually was. We must be willing to look square at the death of self in the death of Christ and then praise our God, and rejoice because of His infinite kindness. Without an open and willing heart to see these hard truths, we cannot be living like Christians. It might be hard to look at, but there can be no victorious resurrection living without the cross and the grave. So read the hard words, but read through them to the hope beyond. Read through it to the joy on the other side. We want hard words and soft hearts.

I have referred throughout this book to the lies that the world is telling us, the false realities they are constantly peddling, the falsehoods we might tell ourselves, or the confusions we have taken on without really noticing.

While they are in fact lies, the real problem is that they haven't *really* deceived us. We adopt them because we have use for them. The fact that we are available to be deceived like this is not an indicator of the trickiness of the lies, but rather a sign of the trickiness of our own hearts. If we didn't want to be lied to, we wouldn't be out in the market of lies looking for good deals. If we didn't want to be lied to, we wouldn't be buying false teaching from "Christian" authors who teach us un-Christian things. On some level we have wanted to be deceived. We have wanted to have things to believe that were not from or in the Word of God. We do not conform our thoughts to the Word, but instead we wait for teaching that does not address our sin honestly. This can *feel* like a good idea to a spiritual coward. I hate to say the obvious, but we should not want to be spiritual cowards, growing in our ability to dodge conviction bullets. Girl, you need to do a lot more than wash your face. This mess is bigger than you can handle, and it's not even cute.

I'll say it again. The fact that false ideas have found places in our lives is not because they were so good and irresistible that we just didn't see they weren't accurate. Sartre did not deceive so many people because he was an *attractive* wall-eyed, five-foot-tall pervert who thought he was being chased by crabs. He deceived people who already wanted to be deceived. When we want to be spoon-fed lies, we are asking to be a child of the devil, nurtured at his knee. Give me more mouthfuls of death, tenderly delivered. Who is the father of lies after all? Not your Father! Go home, Christian, you're drunk on lies.

These lies are actively at work in our lives. They aren't off in the distance. They *all* share common purpose. And almost always we have taken on all this random junk because we are using it for padding between us and God. It is our buffer against the reality of our own situation.

We take in curbside mattresses of bad philosophy and blockade ourselves with them. We snatch up old comforters of worldly platitudes and wrap ourselves up. We duct tape on every bit of padding and secrecy we can find. Never mind that this is all a bunch of flea-filled filth that we have taken out of the world's dumpster. They're futon mattresses from the front of the fraternity, rank with vomit and urine, filth and despair. We are eager to take in almost anything to keep us from seeing the reality of ourselves before God. We're trying to delude ourselves into thinking that He isn't seeing us either. We are always looking for more padding or ways to prevent lines of sight between our nasty selves and our Creator. And we want the comfort of believing it is all accidental and not sinful on our part.

We listen to the teaching of part-time Christians about how to make it all look clean, and they tell us it can feel clean too! It is natural that we have all this here, they say. And this is how people live—stuffed all around with the filth and shame that we call self-empowerment, self-acceptance, insight. We say it is self-esteem and confidence, a journey of self-actualization, but it is just broken down and rejected falsehoods. We were here, eating the baby food of the devil because we were hungry, and we thought this would give us some strength. We want to think this is perfectly normal and there is nothing to see here, nothing to correct or address in our lives. Nothing *wrong*. But there is very little that could be *more* wrong than this situation. Creatures hiding from their Creator. Creatures seeking to be self-sufficient and independent. Creatures broken off from our only source of life, happiness, and being. Children, running to the enemy of our souls for encouragement and help. We have wanted to eat lies but still be true.

When we have peeled back all the layers of confusion and sin that surround our sense of self, we can finally see the heart of the rebellion that we are in. We have to look at the things we have gathered around us for protection and see them as they are. If we love God, we need to turn away from these things and turn to Him. We have to see *us* being seen by Him. There it is—our pitiful self, quivering like the ugly, little mass of worthlessness that it is—and we have to acknowledge what all our lies and confusion are defending, what we are so afraid to see. Here it is, *me*. Here is the thing that I wanted to defend no matter the cost. Here is the little piece of filth that I have loved with an unrighteous love.

We want to be able to love us, as is. We want to be *enough*, but we are profoundly unworthy. We want to go to Heaven, but we deserve

Hell. But God did not save us because we were so valuable. *We have value because He saved us.* There is a world of difference in that, and it's the difference between Heaven and Hell. We want to be able to build ourselves up without Christ, but, at the end, we are only smaller and more wretched. Our miserable little bodies are twisted in confusion, covered in open wounds of pride, blotched with scabs of selfishness and self-importance. We are surrounded by our own filth: our lusts and hatred, our envy of neighbors, our loathing of others, murder in our hearts, and wantonness in our eyes. Here it is, at last, *me.* Worth nothing. Capable of nothing but more filth. Earning nothing but death.

And then, in the glorious words of Ephesians 2:4–10, "But God."

> But God, who is rich in mercy, because of His great love with which He loved us, even when we were dead in trespasses, made us alive together with Christ (by grace you have been saved), and raised *us* up together, and made *us* sit together in the heavenly *places* in Christ Jesus, that in the ages to come He might show the exceeding riches of His grace in His kindness toward us in Christ Jesus. For by grace you have been saved

through faith, and that not of yourselves; *it is* the gift of God, not of works, lest anyone should boast. For we are His workmanship, created in Christ Jesus for good works, which God prepared beforehand that we should walk in them.

We indulge in all this foolishness only to spare ourselves from seeing how merciful our God is, trying to avoid the insult of seeing the exceeding riches of our God: His kindness, His mercy, His great love with which He loved us.

When you are in Christ, you can see your Self (in all its worthlessness) and still laugh with joy. You know the story. This miserable horrible little self *has been shown the exceeding riches of grace and kindness.* This little mass of death and horror has died in Christ, and in Christ is being raised. All the joy, beauty, and soul-crushing glory in the story of this world begins with the ugly worthlessness of fallen sinners, and hinges on the turning point of all of history, "But God."

But God did not accept death for us. *But God* would not leave us dead in our sins. *But God,* because of His great love. *But God,* who is rich in mercy. *But God,* who alone is worthy. *But God,* who is in Heaven. *But God,* who is perfect, and holy, and wise. *But God* looked on you in your horrifying filth, and He gave your filth to Christ. But God gave Christ to you, so that you, in Christ Jesus, can yet live. But God intervened with the blood and body of His Son given for you. But God pulled you away from the devil and his lies, and gives you truth.

Why would God do this? Why would He who is so rich be troubled with us? Why would He care? His creation, lost in sin, is being recreated in His Son. You are His workmanship. You have been created in Christ Jesus *for something*. That something is the good works which He has prepared beforehand for you to walk in. We are not just being recreated, but we are part of the new creation. We are called to walk in the good works that God has prepared for us so that we might be part of bringing about the new creation. We are needed for His purpose. We are part of the plan. We are part of the resolution of this trouble. We are part of the rest of His glorious story, and we have roles in it! We are needed! We were dead in our trespasses, *but God* had a plan for us to not only have life but to be part of bringing about life.

In the flesh we want to protect our death from life. We want to be left alone. *But God*, our Maker, will be our Remaker. He will not let us keep our death, but instead He breaks open our hands and our hearts and fills them with life everlasting. Glorious, free, clean, holy life. His life. The life of His son. This is His body, broken for you. This is His life, given for you. This is His mercy, poured out on you. This is His love, too big to resist. This is your God.

The resurrection is not a happy ending only for Christ. It is the one and only path of life for all people. Christians are given the gift of life in Christ because we were given the great mercy of death in Christ. We died in the One who knew the way back from the grave and would not stay dead. You cannot have resurrection living without the death before it. You cannot have the death of Christ for your sins and then continue to live in them and value them. They are no longer your defining feature. They are no longer your story. They are no longer part of your identity. That old man, to you, is dead. "That you put off, concerning your former conduct, the old man which grows corrupt according to the deceitful lusts, and be renewed in the spirit of your mind, and that you put on the new man which was created according to God, in true righteousness and holiness" (Eph. 4:22).

This is the great wonder of our "already/not yet" faith. The old man has died in Christ, and yet we need to continue to put him off and put on Christ.

We need to choose to follow Christ in our regular lives and daily moments and to walk away from the old man. We know that he has already lost and Christ has won, and yet we need to be continually shaped, continually refined, continually pursuing Christ.

The fact that you still struggle with selfishness and sin and valuing your own will over obedience is not a sign that you have *not* been saved; it is a sign that you *have* been saved. You and the old man are no longer at peace with one another. For as long as we live on earth, we will have this struggle, the struggle of dying to self and living to Christ.

But notice in this passage in Ephesians, Paul is not saying that you put off the old man that you might live in a disembodied way through an all-spiritual existence. You put off the old man that you might put on the new one. You put off the old self that you might put on the new self.

This new self knows God and is not ashamed. This new self can stand before Him in thanksgiving, as a creature worshiping its Creator, as we were meant to be, reflecting His glory and living in His joy. This is what you were created to be. Here there is no shame. Here there is no loneliness. Here there is no neediness. Here there is no longing for something else. Here is Christ, and here is *you*.

NATIVE OF
ANOTHER COUNTRY

"MY SOUL CLINGS TO THE DUST; REVIVE me according to Your word" (Ps. 119:25).

Humans are on the move. We are becoming either one thing or another. We are becoming more Christlike or becoming more worldly. We are either becoming what we were made to be, becoming the truest version of ourselves in our obedience to God, or we are becoming more and more deformed by pursuing and revering anything other than God. We are either hiding from God and being ruined, or running to God and being transformed. There is no middle road—no way of staying uncommitted and un- changing. There is no way of *being* for a human that is not a way of *changing*. We even age in our sleep.

We are hungry little creatures. We need food for the body, and food for the mind, and food for the spirit. We like to consume, and we were made to consume as one of the means of our transformation into the image of Christ. But it makes a great difference what it is we are consuming. Scripture is abundantly clear that it is not through our physical food choic- es that we will be changed for the better. We do not become more like Christ through a re- strictive diet. Jesus said to His disciples when He broke the bread: "This is my body—take and eat." As Christians we are to be partakers of Christ, not abstainers.

But there is another food that the Lord com- mands us to partake of, and that is the Word of God. Many Christians struggle to regular- ly eat at the table of the Word. We know that we are supposed to be reading the Bible, but there is an unbelievable amount of baggage around the issue for many Christians. There are many reasons for this—but I believe centrally it all comes down to the threefold opposition to growth in Christ which we all face—the world, the flesh, and the devil.

The world distracts us (*I am too busy . . . Life is too crazy . . .When I finish watching this . . . When I am done with shopping online . . .*).

The flesh is weak (*I forgot . . . I don't like when I am behind on the reading, so I'll wait until the new year to start again . . . I don't feel like it . . . It sounds like so much work . . .*).

And the devil accuses (*You are the worst Christian . . . How long has it been since you really read the Bible? . . . I can't believe you . . . Everyone else does this, what is wrong with you? . . .*).

It is a shame that so many Christians are kept from the Word by such small obstacles. Part of the reason such little things can keep us away is that we do not rightly estimate the value of regularly reading, *consuming*, the Word of God. We also seem to have drifted into thinking that the Word of God is like a difficult textbook, not food. And so we approach the food as though it is an assignment with the nutrition label, and not a joyful act of obedience and pleasure.

Natural food is an amazing gift. We eat an apple and enjoy the crunch and the taste, and even the sound of a bite snapping off. But we do not continue to evaluate what the apple is doing for us once it is out of sight, nor do we tell it where to go and what to do. This is the kind of simple joy we need to have in coming to the Word. Eat your Bible. Read the Word. Don't try to direct the Word about what you want it to do to you. How could you anyway? Come to this table that your Father has prepared. Pull up a chair and eat. Eat and eat again. Come back tomorrow and eat some more. Sometimes you won't understand what you read, but eat it anyway in joy and gratitude, and it will change you anyway. The very act of eating the Word of God is an act of defining obedience. The Word is alive, and it knows what to do with you even when you don't know what to do with it.

"For the word of God is living and powerful, and sharper than any two-edged sword, piercing even to the division of soul and spirit, and of joints and marrow, and is a discerner of the thoughts and intents of the heart" (Heb. 4:12).

The Word of God also equips us to be right-hearted worshipers, gathering weekly to worship God in the heavenly places, as living stones that are part of His glorious temple. Every Sunday we are conformed through worship more and more into the image of His Son, our chief cornerstone and older brother.

Do you want to be conformed to the image of Christ? Let the Word do it to you. Do you want to overcome the world the flesh and the devil? Let the Word of God and the faithful worship of Him equip you. Do you want to be equipped for every good work? The Word of God will do that for you; the preaching of the Word will strengthen you. Do you want to overcome fear? The Word of God will do that in you.

When we become more like Christ, we are becoming more truly ourselves. The most obedient you is the most *truly you* you. Complete submission to God is complete human fulfillment.

One of the sweet reminders of this truth is that when we have no words—nothing to say to God, He has given us His words. When you open the Psalms and pray with David, you are reading words that are better at expressing *your true self* than any words you could have thought of. When God gave you a new heart, He also made you a native of another country. He gave you a new heart that brought with it new loves, a new homeland, a new people, and a new language.

Have you ever wondered how the words of Scripture can mean so much to you even when you don't really understand them? Like this triumphant refrain from Psalm 24:7a: "Lift up your heads, O you gates! And be lifted up, you everlasting doors!"

Do you know exactly what that means, or what the psalmist meant by the everlasting doors? Probably not. But your heart knows. Your heart soars with the glory–"And the King of glory shall come in. Who is this King of glory? The LORD strong and mighty, the LORD mighty in battle!" (vv. 7b–8).

Your heart knows your King. It knows His glory, and you are gradually learning His language. The more we feast on His words the more we know our own heart's country, the more we learn our own native tongue.

In the Lord's prayer, He taught us to pray, "Thy kingdom come. Thy will be done, on earth as it is in Heaven."

We know that through His Word we are equipped to do His will here. We are equipped to do the good works that He has prepared for those of us who are called according to His purpose. This is the work He has for us: that we speak His language here, that we live His story here, that we be thoroughly, completely, obediently, His people here, and that we go about our daily lives planting flags for our homeland, claiming all the territories that we encounter here for His kingdom. We claim our busy days and our tired nights for the kingdom. We claim our lawn work and our work days. We claim our meal prep and our pregnancies for Christ. We plant Kingdom flags in every place our hands find work and in every place our hearts find trouble. We claim all of Christ for all of life, forever.

"Now the God of peace, that brought again from the dead our Lord Jesus, that great shepherd of the sheep, through the blood of the everlasting covenant, make you perfect in every good work to do his will, working in you that which is well pleasing in his sight, through Jesus Christ; to whom be glory for ever and ever. Amen" (Heb. 13:20–21, KJV).

CPSIA information can be obtained
at www.ICGtesting.com
Printed in the USA
BVHW081036270519
549345BV00030B/2837/P